Big Business:

A NEW ERA

Books by the same author

❧

TVA: DEMOCRACY ON THE MARCH

THIS I DO BELIEVE

Big Business:
A NEW ERA

BY

David E. Lilienthal

HARPER & BROTHERS
PUBLISHERS   NEW YORK

TO HELEN

CONTENTS

AUTHOR'S NOTE   ix

ACKNOWLEDGMENTS   xiii

PART I. A NEW ERA OF OPPORTUNITY

1. FEELINGS VERSUS FACTS ABOUT BIGNESS   3
2. BIG BUSINESS IN A CHANGED AMERICA   13
3. BIG BUSINESS FOR A BIG COUNTRY   31

PART II. BIGNESS AND THE NEW COMPETITION

4. BIGNESS—THE LIFE OF TRADE   47
5. COMPETITION—BETWEEN THE "OBJECTS
   OF DESIRE"   58
6. MODERN RESEARCH AND COMPETITION   68
7. COMPETITION THROUGH DIVERSIFICATION   73
8. COMPETITION AND INTEGRATION   81
9. COMPETITION AND THE ONE BIG MARKET   88
10. INTERNAL COMPETITION   91
11. ADVERTISING AND COMPETITION   93

Contents

PART III. THE FRUITS OF BIGNESS

	INTRODUCTION	97
12.	BIGNESS FOR NATIONAL SECURITY	98
13.	BIGNESS FOR INDIVIDUAL SECURITY	105
14.	PRODUCTIVITY AND BIGNESS	109
15.	BIGNESS AND THE DISTRIBUTION OF GOODS AND CREDIT	114
16.	BIGNESS AND CONSERVATION OF NATURAL RESOURCES	122

PART IV. THE HAZARDS OF BIGNESS

17.	NEW WORRIES FOR OLD	133
18.	CONCENTRATION OF POWER: "TOO BIG TO HANDLE"	138
19.	CENTRALIZATION AND BIGNESS	151
20.	TOO BIG: THE DANGERS OF INEFFICIENCY, STERILITY AND BUREAUCRACY	156

PART V. A NEW POLICY TOWARD BIGNESS: FROM NO TO YES

21.	TRUST BUSTING: DOES IT MAKE SENSE TODAY?	167
22.	A PROPOSAL: A BASIC ECONOMIC LAW	181
23.	MAKING BIGNESS SERVE MODERN INDIVIDUALISM	189
	INDEX	205

AUTHOR'S NOTE

This is a book about the creativeness of America in the mid-twentieth century, and the new era this creativeness is bringing into being. More specifically it is about present-day Big Business as a fresh manifestation of American imagination and vitality.

My conviction about Big Business, as expressed through-out this book, is that it represents a proud and fruitful achievement of the American people as a whole; that in Big Business we have more than an efficient way to produce and distribute basic commodities, and to strengthen the nation's security; we have a social institution that promotes human freedom and individualism.

Big Business, as it has now evolved, far from being an evil and a menace, provides an opportunity to build the physical basis for an even stronger democracy and an even greater people; it was in this sense that Walt Whitman wrote of "riches, and the getting of riches, and the amplest products, power, activity, inventions, movements, etc." as the "substrata" upon which he would "raise the edifice" of his Democratic Vistas for the future of his country.

I am by no means a worshiper of Bigness for its own sake, either in government or in business. My oft-expressed conviction that "Big Government is not inevitable" finds concrete expression in the TVA, as a demonstration of decentralization of Federal functions to the states and local communities. My belief that small business has an essential economic and human role in American life is attested by more than thirteen years of effort to help in the creation and nurturing of private small business in the Tennessee Valley. And, as I point out in this book, one of the most attractive aspects of modern Big Business is that it creates opportunities previously nonexistent for a multitude of small business enterprises, and broadens the area wherein smaller businesses can find opportunities that are neither profitable nor suitable for the big.

Nor is my theme based upon ignoring or condoning the ignoble pages of the history of Big Business. These past derelictions are vivid in my memory, and toward the correction of some of the most noisome abuses I had a not inactive part.

It seems to me quite natural and appropriate that this frankly enthusiastic and optimistic view of Big Business should be written by one who has spent most of his adult life as an administrator of huge public enterprises. It was my job to deal with business, big and small, solely on the basis of what it could do to further the public welfare. As a consequence, the ways in which Big Business actually does bring public benefits (to a description of which much of this book is devoted) became more evident to me than they might have been to those whose work has been primarily with private business.

It is government's changed and expanded role in economic affairs, notably since 1933, that in my opinion reduces to quite manageable proportions the danger of abuses by Big Business: thus armed we can now safely promote and encourage Bigness rather than view its growth with apprehension. It seems natural enough that one who participated in bringing about some of these changes might see more clearly their implications as protection against corporate abuse than had he been in private life during those years.

The convictions about Big Business presented in this book grew out of more than twenty years of experience, observation and reflection. Many times during those years I had to revise my opinions and prejudgments because they simply did not square with the facts as I found them to be.

Similarly, many readers may approach the thesis of this book with their minds already made up, disagreeing, perhaps violently, with my conclusions about Big Business, or my estimate of the constructive role of modern government, or the contributions to democracy made by organized labor. It is my hope that they, too, will be prepared to take a new, fresh and relaxed look at these controversial issues; that in this process they will find—as over the years I found—some of the keen satisfaction that comes to those who pursue the often uncomfortable but always rewarding experience of seeking to make one's views, and especially one's emotions, fit the facts of the world as it actually is.

It is in the ancient liberal faith—to which the writer is committed—that our course be governed not by the dead hand of yesterday's facts and prejudices but by the living realities of today and our aspirations for tomorrow. It is this genius for making change serve the eternal unchanging values we cherish that is the very essence of American liberalism.

In this book I write primarily of Bigness in business. But what I have in the back of my mind is more than the need for realism, honest emotion and sensible public policy about Big Business. We are ready for a new frame of mind about our newborn industrial civilization and its potentialities for the development of the individual personality. The time is right. There is the feel of change in the wind.

DAVID E. LILIENTHAL

23 Beekman Place
New York City
October 20, 1952

ACKNOWLEDGMENTS

For their careful reading and discerning criticism of the manuscript of this book I am indebted to a number of economists, and in particular to Dr. J. Frederic Dewhurst and Dr. Simon N. Whitney of the staff of the Twentieth Century Fund, to my daughter, Mrs. Sylvain Bromberger of Cambridge, Massachusetts, and to Mr. Frederick D. Forsch, of New York City. Although we were not always in complete agreement, their comments were most helpful and clarifying. I wish also to express my special thanks to Mr. James Derieux, chief of the Washington bureau of *Collier's* Magazine, to Mr. Joseph Volpe, Jr., of the District of Columbia bar, and to Mrs. James T. Walden of Washington for their assistance and encouragement.

Only by reason of my wife's patience, understanding and the hard labor of editorial assistance over many months was it possible for me to write this book in the midst of the heavy demands of my business activities. The dedication of the book to her is a wholly inadequate expression of my immeasurable gratitude, esteem and affection.

A portion of this book appeared, in somewhat different form and sequence, as a series of articles in *Collier's* Magazine in May and June, 1952.

D.E.L.

PART I

A NEW ERA OF OPPORTUNITY

1

Feelings versus Facts
about Bigness

I F WE are to understand the United States today, if
we are to develop a conviction about her future, we
must fully comprehend that Big Business is basic to the
very life of this country; and yet many—perhaps most—
Americans have a deep-seated fear and an emotional
repugnance to it. Here is a monumental contradiction.

It is toward a change in our feeling about Bigness and
a resolution of this contradiction that this book is directed.
For without such a change in sentiment the creative pos-
sibilities of Bigness in economic affairs cannot be fully
realized and put to their best and highest uses.

It is therefore necessary at the very outset to recognize
how important a part emotions play in the creation of the
economic and legal policies by which we deal with Big
Business in this country and how, as a consequence of
these emotions, the actual benefits of Bigness are often
expressly dismissed as "irrelevant."

One might expect such a surrender to feeling and economic prejudice in political debates and campaign speeches. But it is not so restricted. Indeed, the classic current exposition of a frankly emotional antagonism to Bigness was formulated in the highest court of the land.*

The actual economic and social *consequences* of Bigness —whether for evil or for the public interest—are not given rational consideration when rhetorical indignation and dogmatism obscure the issue.

The ill effect of rejecting the facts is not limited to Big Business. Fear, suspicion and emotional distrust of large business have inevitably created a degree of cynical distrust of *all* business, and a downgrading of the businessman's function in society.

To safeguard ourselves against conclusions based upon prejudgments and feeling, it is of the greatest importance that we scrutinize coolly the actual operation in the daily lives of men of this great institution of America in the mid-twentieth century. We need fully to understand its benefits to us. We need to be seeking ways by which it may be improved.

We need to be aware of the consequences to us of a continuation of these lingering antagonisms and suspicions of another day, these backward glances at a time that is past and gone. This feeling brings a host of evil consequences in its wake. It acts as a drag upon our economic headway. It slows down our social and political progress. It largely accounts for a defensive, partisan and often quite negative attitude in public affairs on the part of many busi-

* See the dissenting opinion of Mr. Justice Douglas in U.S. v. Columbia Steel Co. (1948) 334 U.S. 495, 534, 537.

ness leaders who have every reason to be affirmative and every need to be constructive. It breeds envy and hatred to contaminate the air of American social relations. It shunts the discussion of economic policy from qualified, serious men to ignorant and unscrupulous demagogues and the superficial ghost-thinkers and slogan-writers of business, labor and politics.

As a further consequence of this refusal to give honest recognition to the actual benefits of Big Business—to the individual and to the country—under the new conditions of today, the basic governmental business policies and the everyday enforcement of the antitrust laws are still based largely upon prejudice created by abuses long since corrected, upon an antiquarian's portrait of another America, not the America of the mid-twentieth century. The legal antagonism to size as such causes a profligate waste and distraction of the energies of management and technical talent of business. It substitutes, in business councils, the supercaution, not to say timidity, of the lawyer for the enterprise and boldness of a business manager and technical expert. It bogs down the Federal courts with endless and unmanageable litigation to the detriment of all other litigants. Because much of our public policy toward Big Business and its expression in interminable antitrust lawsuits and Congressional investigations is so obviously fruitless and barren, it thereby undermines respect for government among conscientious citizens.

The emotional responses upon which much business governmental policy rests proceed upon the assumption that small-unit business still should be, or can be, the norm. Thus, one who has had a most important role in shaping government policy concerning size writes:

. . . Judge Hand's system of small producers is once again to be preferred to a system of monopolistic combines. The promotion of managerial incentive is still, I think, in line with the Latin maxim: "Better first man in a little Iberian village, than second in Rome." The wellsprings of economic democracy and advance are better maintained in an economic society where Thorstein Veblen's political sentiments of local autonomy and insubordination prevail. . . .*

As a consequence of emotional preference for a "system of small producers" the burden has been put on Big Business to *disprove* that its growth and success are evidence of real or potential injury to the commonwealth.

But today small-scale business, while it is an integral, essential part of our society, is certainly *not* the norm. The driving force of our economic life is now large business; no amount of nostalgia for the good old days can change that fact.

What chiefly stands in the way of the fuller realization of the great productive and social benefits of Bigness is, then, *a way of thinking*. We think negatively. We are preoccupied with restraints, prohibitions, antitrust, antimonopoly, anti-this and anti-that. This should not be the mood of sanguine and confident Americans.

We seem to be split personalities, against Bigness but desiring its fruits. But we can't have it completely both

* "Some Justification for Divestiture," by Mr. Sigmund Timberg, until recently Chief, Judgment and Judgment Enforcement Section, Antitrust Division, Department of Justice, in *George Washington Law Review*, December, 1950.

ways. We cannot try, at one and the same time, to restore the past and to create the future. As a nation, we can't live in a world of economic folk dancing and basket weaving and simultaneously in the world of the big productive machine.

I believe that we should set about at once to re-examine the outdated structure of our feeling, our thinking and our public policy toward Bigness. We should, in my opinion, replace it with a foundation of feeling and of economic and legal policy based upon the realities of the mid-twentieth century. The times call for a rousing affirmation that Bigness can be made the means of promoting and furthering not only our nation's productivity but more important still the freedom and the well-being of its individual citizens.

To this proposition, the question might reasonably be asked: "Why do we need to do anything to encourage Bigness? Look at the great corporations that have grown up, and continue to grow. Isn't this proof that our policies have not hurt the country and have not hurt Bigness?"

The answer depends partly upon whether one conceives of America as now at the height of her powers and growth, or only at the beginning, with her greatest potentialities yet to be realized, the greatest test of productiveness yet to come. I believe the latter to be the case.

That Big Business has performed economic wonders with one hand tied behind its back by our suspicions and fears does not mean that these handicaps do not exist. It only foreshadows what it could do working with both hands, in an affirmative atmosphere, one that recognizes its capabilities and achievements.

We are not, as some say, "at the end of an era." We are at the *beginning* of an era, one in which Bigness—encouraged, not hobbled—can fulfill its promise of benefits.

Our huge chemical industry and our vast industries based upon petroleum are both still infants, in age and size. Electronics, big as it is, is in knee pants, its future growth and potentialities unlimited. Electronic devices for many purposes will become as familiar in the factory, office and home as radio and television sets.

Our production and processing of food, our lumbering and coal mining, our shoe and clothing, furniture, fertilizer, textile and pharmaceutical industries have hardly begun to use the advantages of the techniques of large-scale enterprise.

The air-cooling of American homes has reached major proportions, but actually it has hardly begun, measured by the demand and need; less than 10 per cent of commercial buildings and an even lesser percentage of factories are equipped to assure this modern minimum of human comfort and business efficiency.

Moreover, a whole new world of industrial energy and radiation will come from the peaceful atom.

The disastrous floods in the Missouri Valley are a national disgrace to a country as advanced in water and soil technology as we are. The Missouri can be tamed and put to work if we make up our minds to do the job. Cleaning up the pollution of the rivers of the Atlantic seaboard, ridding the atmosphere over our great cities of noxious fumes, smog and smoke, converting the salty waters of the sea, by economic industrial-sized processes, into potable water for irrigation of arid land are but examples of big jobs for Bigness.

A fantastic transformation can come about if we go at our housing opportunities through Bigness. Our need for many new hospitals and training centers runs into billions of dollars. The public schools alone have capital needs representing many billions in buildings and equipment.

Remaking our highways from coast to coast will be one of the greatest construction undertakings in history. Providing ample modern parking facilities and motor terminals is another giant undertaking urgently needed.

Our city streets are congested, beyond comfort and good economics. They need to be widened, elevated, modernized. This can be done if we go at the job with the advantages of Bigness to help us, and with the boldness, sense and integrity of men like New York City's Robert Moses to plan and direct the work.

The free nations now depend on us for military might, for "economic aid" and for our strengthening influence in a world rocking with fear and unrest. If our economic system should falter or fail, the whole free world would be shaken to its foundations. To maintain this position of leadership is costly; it requires sustained and ever-increasing American productivity.

Here at home what the American people have come to expect and to demand of their economic system has also reached new heights. Our demands upon our productive system in the future will be even greater.

These are the political and economic realities with which we must deal.

The American economy has undergone a major reformation, during two wars and a prolonged depression. In its fundamentals, however, as a going concern, it remains strong and dynamic and essentially capitalistic.

If this modern kind of capitalistic system is to continue to be healthy there must constantly be generated the need for the investment and use of new capital. Such needs grow out of new ideas. Consequently, research, technical development, invention and industrial and social innovation have become necessary conditions of a healthy expanding capitalism, American style.

A quick sure way to bring about economic stagnation and an end to the dynamic, expanding quality of our society is to permit the springs of scientific research and development to dry up. From these springs flow technological change whereby whole new industries, such as television, come into being, and an existing industry, such as chemicals, is able to double (as it did) in little more than a decade.

For this and other reasons it is therefore in the interest of small business, as well as large, to help create favorable conditions for big research in industry, in universities and in government, and to assure ample private incentives for the *industrial translation* of these technical developments into new and improved products, so that individual savings will flow into these new developments.

We can meet both domestic and international demands upon our productive capacity, but only if we make full use of our talent for the large-scale organization and administration of industry, research, distribution, credit, conservation of resources.

The foundation on which this twentieth-century economic and social policy can be built must evolve from a growing knowledge of the facts and the *meaning* of the facts that bear on the advantages of Bigness in the everyday life of everyday Americans.

We need a set of measuring rods by which to judge our business institutions, and what it is we want and expect of business. We need to determine, on the basis of the facts, whether and to what extent the technique of Bigness has succeeded, in specific situations, in giving us what we want; to what extent and under what circumstances the encouragement of Bigness is in the public interest; what new public safeguards we may require, what existing ones are self-defeating, ineffectual and outmoded.

In this process of analysis we need the continued research and findings of our leading universities and economic foundations, institutions such as the Twentieth Century Fund, the Ford Foundation, the Committee for Economic Development, the Brookings Institution, the research divisions of our national labor organizations, the Business Advisory Council of the Department of Commerce, and many others.

These various inquiries should not concentrate almost exclusively (as in so many past inquiries) upon potential or actual dangers and abuses; they should also try to measure the *beneficial effect of Bigness,* as judged by such criteria as these:

1. Does Bigness increase and stimulate competition between ideas, products or services, and thereby provide additional areas of free choice for consumers and producers?

2. Does it increase the funds and the human energy expended, per unit of products or sales, on basic or applied research and development, toward improvement of products, new and more diverse products, better management techniques, greater conservation of materials, greater use of machinery, greater safety or health of workers—and kindred objectives?

3. Does Bigness strengthen constructive labor-management relations and collective bargaining, further mutual responsibility and sharing of benefits of increased productivity, increase individual satisfactions for workers and managers?

4. Does it produce greater stability of employment, industry by industry, and business by business, on a *year-round* basis?

5. Does it increase industrial output per dollar of capital invested and man hour of labor expended?

6. Does Bigness increase and fortify competition by adding to the number of large units capable of effective competition with other existing large units of industry?

7. Does it strengthen competition by making available to producers new or alternative sources of raw or semifinished materials?

8. Does Bigness promote and further a maximum of managerial decentralization, delegation of authority and geographical decentralization?

9. Does it promote industrial diversification?

10. Does Bigness promote conservation of natural resources?

11. Does Big Business result in the creation of hitherto nonexistent opportunities for new independent businesses?

12. Has Bigness effectively concerned itself with the individual, his freedom, his well-being, his opportunity to grow and develop?

It is to such questions as these, rather than to the intricacies of economic theory, the refinements of antitrust law or the abstractions of political argument that the inquiry embodied in this book is directed.

2

Big Business in a Changed America

IN THE past twenty-five years profound changes have taken place in this country in virtually every area of our lives as individuals and as a people. This inquiry into the place of Big Business in America would be abstract and without reality unless projected against the background of these changes.

The New Role of Government

Of these changes since the twenties none is more pervasive and none more relevant to the issue of Big Business than the changes in the function and role of government.

Government has become an active and frequently the dominant factor in economic affairs. Today few important decisions are made by business executives and boards of directors in which some of the acts of government do not play a significant part. What is true of businessmen also applies, generally, to farmers and workers in industry.

Most of us, thus far, have only dimly comprehended how completely this change has affected the conduct of business, farming, and government, nor do we realize clearly, as yet, how direct a bearing this has upon our views and convictions about Big Business.

Depending upon one's viewpoint or economic interest, the broadened function of modern government is bemoaned as the end of our liberties, or applauded as progress. The important fact, in this present inquiry, is that it is an accomplished fact, a fact upon which current plans and future policies must be built. However much emotional resistance there may be to government's new role, in the abstract—and it is very considerable—when it comes down to meeting specific problems, the public now expects and often demands that government have a considerable hand in economic matters. There is no indication whatever that in the coming decade this expanded role of government will be abandoned; such changes as occur will likely be only in degree and in choice of methods.

When a drought burns up pastures over a wide area as it did in the summer of 1952, when a mining company or a hospital is unable to borrow money privately on favorable terms, when longshoremen or garbage collectors or steel workers cannot agree with their employers, when farmers find the market for their cotton or hogs is slipping, Americans, sometimes wisely, sometimes unwisely, look to their government. When there is too much of any commodity at any given time—potatoes, for example—or not enough, such as the mineral tantalum, when prices are too high for customers or too low for merchandisers, when bank depositors become uneasy about their deposits, when manufacturers find inventories of appliances are piling up and their distributors feel that installment credit should be easier—in these and hundreds of other familiar situations between buyer and seller, between employer and employee, between landlord and tenant, between borrower and lender, between insurer and insured, between one geographic group or region and another, government now has a significant role. Machinery will be set up where it is not already now available for government participation in many economic relationships and transactions which forty years ago, or less, were regarded as strictly private matters to be determined by the impersonal forces of economic power in the hands of the parties to the transactions.

Some of these measures, of course, are "temporary" or for a particular "emergency" (though some "temporary" measures have arrived at their second decade). Making all qualifications, however, I think no one would seriously assert that *taken as a whole* this change in the role of government is not here to stay, or that we shall ever return to the scope of government of the twenties. Most of us want the job done better, or differently; I, for one, should earnestly hope that there will be a greater healthy emphasis upon local government and a decentralization of many Federal functions. But for all the refusal, emotionally, to embrace the new kind of America, we do find on all sides an *expectation* that it will continue.

The change that has come about in the vital area of banking, finance and credit is one of the most marked of any in the whole array of transformations in our economic life. The often-quoted aphorism that the seat of financial power, since 1933, has "moved from Wall Street to Washington" is more colorful than accurate. But certain it is that, along with the whole financial community (and not alone the bankers in New York), Washington has now greatly increased influence in credit and finance, and action there determines most of the broad assumptions upon which private finance proceeds. For it is Washington that determines the principal facts underlying private financial decisions—the size of our enormous public expenditures and the size and distribution of the burden of taxes. It is in Washington that the volume, character and timing of new government securities is determined, the conditions under which commercial banking proceeds, the circumstances under which securities of most corporations may be offered for sale in the public capital markets, and many others of the factors which influence or fix the timing, rate and character of private financing.

The part played by government, however, is only one element in the deep change in the world of finance. Credit to individuals and to economic enterprise has become one of the most highly competitive parts of American business, and one with the greatest diversity. Finance is now actively engaged in by commercial banks, savings and loan associations, insurance companies, co-operatives, federal land banks, the R.F.C., industrial credit unions, savings banks, personal loan companies and so on. Indeed, the battle cries of Populism, "banker monopoly" and the "money trust," have gone out of the vernacular because they have disappeared from the world of reality.

To sum up, then: the role of government in virtually every single aspect of American life has undergone profound and thoroughgoing changes, changes that must be kept vividly in mind as a major premise in any consideration of Big Business as it is today.

The Changed Role of Organized Labor

The new place of power and influence of organized industrial workers in the economic and political life of America, in the new era since 1933, is of course so well known as to require little more than a listing in this enumeration of changes.

The all-powerful tyrannic employer is all but gone. Gone too, except for historians, is the picture of workers who must endure long hours of labor, with no vacations, no decent opportunity to have their grievances heard, no chance to join unions openly because their employer forbids it, no concern for their individual aspirations and special aptitudes. Gone too are the abuses of company stores, child labor, "yellow-dog contracts."

Even more significant a change than these minus marks are certain affirmative facts.

Foremost among these, according to my observation, is this: workers and their unions are generally almost as strongly committed, emotionally, to free enterprise as a system and to the financial success of the business in which they work as are their supervisors and executives. Certainly "class war" between employees and owners—a not unconventional idea in many labor circles only a generation ago—is as dated and outmoded as the livery stable and the "family entrance." Labor disputes are with us still of course, some of them bitter and often terribly costly; and strikes and work stoppages we shall always have, so long as we remain a free people. But the spirit in which even the most hotly contested strikes are carried on shows, in many small incidents, how deep we have buried the class-war philosophy. A company makes a point of paying striking employees, on the picket line, vacation pay due them, or serves pickets hot coffee, since they are "our employees and will be back at work one of these days"; a surge of exceptional production per man often characterizes the first weeks on the job after a strike. Many other such instances could be cited to show that for all their differences about pay and union status, and for all the strong language used, the workers and their unions feel they are part of their industry. And the individual skilled factory workman, with his car and bowling league and a vacation cabin at the lake and perhaps a son in college, is like most any other middle-group citizen in the essential stability and conservatism of his basic economic and political views.

For long years it was quite common for individual workers and their union leadership to oppose the introduction of "labor-saving" machinery, superior technology that upset established craft skills, and scientific management techniques. Typesetters fought the first linotype machines; farm workers even burned the early wheat "combines." The history of labor relations for generations has been marked by acts of violence against better machinery or management methods; this might have meant, if continued, an end to increased productivity, a catastrophe as reactionary as it is inhumane. In the past twenty years in some of our greatest industries this antagonism has greatly ameliorated. Indeed, powerful labor leaders such as John L. Lewis of the Mine Workers and Walter Reuther of the Auto Workers pride themselves on their aid to mechanization.

Here again is an affirmative fact, a change for which we need to thank our lucky stars and our essential good sense.

The fact is that better machinery and constantly new and improved processes and management offer far greater promise of higher returns for capital and workers than the old-time methods of pressure upon workers by the boss, and pressure on the boss by workers. If such conviction becomes widespread—and there is a good chance that it may —it will do more to advance the cause of social peace and harmony, and put it on a solid foundation, than all the bitter rows, the dramatic legislative battles and the emotional pyrotechnics on both sides that have marked the course of our progress toward maturity in human relations in industry.

But of course in the labor field the most significant change is in a modification of the power of employers to fix the terms and conditions of employment. Collective bargaining covering most aspects of employment has become an accepted fact throughout almost the whole of big industry. What were once matters to be determined solely by the employer are now matters of negotiation and agreement with labor's representatives. This represents, realistically, nothing less than a diffusion in the power of decision in the most important elements of industrial affairs, as contrasted with the concentration of such power in the hands of management.

If for no other reason (and there are many others) than this new power of organized labor the reasons for fear of corporate Bigness today bear little resemblance to those that existed in 1910 or 1916 or even 1932.

This new power of labor by some is seen as a long step backward; by others (I certainly count myself among them) as, on the whole, great democratic progress. The significant thing, however, is that the change is accepted as a working fact. Those who expect labor unions to be destroyed or drastically weakened (and of this there was much talk, hopeful or fearful, only a few years ago) are now regarded as unrealistic or alarmists. There are many battles ahead over organized labor, many abuses and inadequacies that need correction. But there seems no prospect that the issue about organized labor will ever again become one of its life or death.

The Change in Our National
Security Needs: the Arms Race

Another important change, necessary to an understanding of the place of Bigness in present-day America, is often
passed over, so far as its economic consequences are concerned, on the ground that it is a "temporary" or "emergency" condition. I refer to the state of tension between the
Soviet Union and the United States and its friends of the
free world, tensions that are forcing us to rearm at a furious
pace.

The occasion for this arms program bears no resemblance
whatever to the occasional acute commercial rivalries, differences over territory or general testiness between nations
which in the past have been described as "international tension." The antagonism between ourselves and Communist
Russia is not only real; it is concerned with our vital interests and deepest convictions, and theirs. Accordingly, vague
cheeriness that some magic formula of disarmament will be
devised to wipe away the clouds in the foreseeable future
is shallow and insubstantial. We must instead face the
probability not of war but of a prolonged period in which
we shall need to be heavily armed. As prudent people with
everything at stake, we must count on maintaining a substantial military establishment which will absorb millions
of our manpower. We shall be forced, so far as anyone now
can foresee, to hold a lead in the race for new scientific
weapons, requiring the greatest of technical and industrial
resources and prowess. We shall be faced with huge out-

lays to aid other nations allied with us in this war that is not called war.

Such a prolonged armament race is a great change for us. We have done this sort of thing for a quick spurt, when we found ourselves in a declared and "conventional" war. But we have no precedent or experience in continuing such a state of arming and aid—even at a half of the astounding rate for the fiscal year 1953 of $57 billion a year—for ten, perhaps fifteen years.

The issue of Big Business cannot be intelligently thought about if our need for Bigness to attain a measure of security is not given major and preponderant weight. To this issue I shall return more specifically at a later point in this book; certainly it must be listed high on the roster of profound change in America.

The Change in the Power of Decision of the Owners and Managers of Large Corporate Enterprise

There is no more striking evidence of the revolutionary change that has come over the life of America in the past two to three decades than the change in the prerogative of directors and officers to exercise economic power over the fortunes of a big enterprise.

The term "economic power" as applied to the directors and officers of a corporation means simply the power to decide how the business is to be run. This would include, of course, such matters as wages and working conditions and hours of labor, and pensions and vacations, all of which expenditures so largely determine the cost of the products; what products the company shall make, the quality of those products and the prices to be charged for them; by what means and how much capital should be raised; what should be paid for the use of the money thus borrowed or subscribed and for the banking services employed to find the capital, the types of securities to be issued and their price and conditions—and so on down the list of the many other important decisions which must be made in the operation of a large corporate business.

For many decades the economic power to run the business of a corporation, while far from absolute, was very broad indeed. It was in such a setting of almost complete say-so by corporate officers and directors over the management of business that the antitrust laws of this country came into being (the Sherman Antitrust Act in 1890) and were strengthened (notably the Clayton Act in 1914). Why it appeared so vital in 1890 and 1914 to preserve competition is certainly clear enough when it is recalled that at that time competition was virtually the *sole* limitation upon the economic power of nonutility industrial enterprises of great size.

A few months before the election of Franklin Roosevelt in November of 1932 there was published a book dealing with the concentration of economic power in the hands of very large corporations. This book, *The Modern Corporation and Private Property* by Adolf A. Berle, Jr., and Gardiner C. Means (Macmillan, 1932), had a great impact upon the thinking and the policy making of the country. The figures there brought together for the first time showed quite clearly that in basic industries private individual enterprise had been replaced by group or corporation enterprise; that ownership of huge corporations was for the most part diffused into many hands rather than closely held by a relatively few "owners" or families, with a consequent separation between management and ownership.

The authors concluded that the two hundred largest corporations "control nearly half the corporate wealth" of the country. "This concentration is made even more significant," they wrote, "when it is recalled that as a result of it, approximately 2,000 individuals out of a population of 125,000,000 are in a position to control and direct half of industry" (p. 33). This picture of concentration of economic power was rendered even more startling to the country by this additional comment: "Production is carried on under the ultimate control of a handful of individuals. . . . Approximately 2,000 men were directors of the 200 largest corporations in 1930. Since an important part of these are inactive, the ultimate control of nearly half of industry was actually in the hands of a few hundred men."

The Berle-Means study appeared when the great depression of 1929 was about at its depth, and just as the Presidential election—the Roosevelt-Hoover contest—was opening.

Whether the picture Berle and Means drew was explicitly accurate, in a technical sense, or whether their economic conclusions were sound has, of course, been questioned. But the important thing is that *at the time* they were quite widely accepted.*

* For Professor Berle's present views on Bigness see his article, "The Developing Law of Corporate Concentration," *University of Chicago Law Review*, Vol. 19, Summer, 1952, p. 639, in the opening paragraph of

Moreover, their conclusion—that effective, absolute economic power was in a few hands—became a part of the emotional setting and the economic and political thinking of segments of the country at a time of great upheaval. Because of its timing and its authorship this study had important and immediate practical consequences in the world of action.

In the same summer in which he wrote the final words of this book (July, 1932) Professor Berle became a principal member of the Brain Trust assembled by Franklin Roosevent prior to his election to prepare a proposed legislative program. The result, largely enacted into law in 1933, proved to be the most extensive and far-reaching single reformation of the American system since the Articles of Confederation were supplanted by the Constitution. The change was not, however, like the adoption of the Constitution, chiefly a political, that is to say governmental, transformation. The New Deal laws, taken in their often contradictory entirety, affected fundamentally not only our governmental but also our economic structure.

This was only a matter of twenty years ago. Today the degree of actual control and "absolutism" that remains in the hands of the directors and officers of the largest American corporations has changed almost beyond recognition.

I shall not reargue the old statistical chestnut: has "con-

---

which, for example, he states that the "exigency of technical development has favored vastly increased size and scope of the corporate enterprise. This has been powerfully aided by the system of distribution dependent on national markets. Great size in many crucial fields thus becomes advantageous."

centration of corporate economic power" in large companies since that time increased or diminished or remained about the same? There are responsible advocates for each position. What is important as a practical matter is that the meaning and content of "corporate economic power" has changed completely; it has been so watered down that it is hardly recognizable as "economic power." It certainly is not that "new form of absolutism" of which Berle wrote in 1932 (p. 124).

In short, as a result of the new comprehensive role of government in economic affairs, the new power and influence of organized labor, the rise of the New Competition (largely based upon research, as I shall indicate in a later chapter), a change in the power of large *buyers*—Sears, Roebuck, General Motors, etc.—and most of all a change as to the social responsibility of Big Business (in the public mind and that of its management as well), corporate control, far from being a virtual absolute in the majority of directors or stockholders, is now divided and *diffused*. This is fundamental to a consideration of Big Business today.

Perhaps as good a way as any to make graphic and concrete the effect of these changes from the 1932 picture of the "economic autocrats" is to consider rather fully the change in the sense of social responsibility of top management of Big Business today.

This change is more than a negative matter, the virtual disappearance of the tycoon and the capitalist, of the newspaper cartoons so familiar in the years prior to the Great Depression. There is an *affirmative* fact, highly relevant to

any consideration of Big Business and of a new appraisal
of the validity and relevance of the old fears of Bigness.
There is a decided trend—"trend" is perhaps not a strong
enough word to describe it—to a new kind of "top boss"
of large business undertakings. He is a man with a strong
and practical sense of responsibility to the public, and an
awareness of the ethics of present-day business competition.
Coupled with this trend, is the great increase in top managers who have been trained, as professional men, in the
now numerous and seasoned graduate schools of business
administration. Then, too, there are the newer type of
executives who have come to management posts with a
background of technical training and experience, as
chemists, chemical engineers, physicists, mechanical or
civil engineers, or have been promoted from specialized
technical posts, such as experts in the technology of textiles
or glass or petroleum.

These men represent graphically, in their persons and
in their outlook and function, the coming of age of Big
Business.

Business-management ability is the most pragmatic
of all skills. Only those practitioners who can get results
are regarded as successful. Therefore, the president of a
large enterprise who does not know how to guide his company so it can live and make profits and grow in the changed
America of the mid-century is, almost by definition, a
failure. Rightly or wrongly, there is not too much sympathy for top management that has chronically antagonistic
relations with government or with the public. Whatever
the merits of the controversy, a large company constantly

involved in labor disputes and resulting work stoppages is not generally regarded among important customers or among large investment groups as a good company to buy from or to invest in. The job of management is to produce results in accordance with the practical code of the world of business: "Moral victories" for their companies, at the cost of sales or competitive position or profits are not highly valued.

Moreover, large business undertakings are now responsible to so many different and diverse interests that the job of running such a company has come to be more nearly like that of a public official than that of a traditional business owner or manager.

There was a time when it was considered that a business management was doing its job if it satisfied its owners and its customers. Then later the company's employees and their union representatives were added to the list of those who had in some way to be satisfied or mollified.

Now, however, for many large enterprises the boss has a far more complex problem even than this. Ownership has become widely diffused; the ownership of most such companies is not predominantly in the hands of the founder, or his family, or a banking group. Large stock ownership by huge open-end investment trusts, insurance companies, endowment funds, foundations and pension funds is more and more increasing the groups to which a company president is accountable.

To a lesser but increasing degree the widespread ownership by the general public of the common stock of Big Business provides top management with more and more "bosses." The fact that the management of most large corporations must now make "inside" information available to the public adds to the number that management must satisfy, or whose criticism it must be prepared to answer.

But even all this describes only the broadened responsibility of Big Business management to its "owners." Customers have become more and more conscious of the influence they can exert to get what they want. This is by no means true only of buyers of huge quantities, such as chain stores or automobile companies. Even a routine price increase, that must have seemed to the steel companies a matter of their "private business," not long ago created such a furor among purchasers generally that it was necessary for steel's management to justify its prices before a joint Congressional committee. The full light—even the glare—of nationwide publicity played upon this routine business action, something which a generation ago would have been unthinkable.

Not only a big company's prices are thus the subject of public challenge and criticism if not actual fixing—as in the case of government stockpiling, or regulation of milk prices, or price ceilings. The same is true of the quality of its products; its labor relations; whether it discriminates between white and Negro employees or customers; whether fumes from its stacks, or its wage scales, have a bad effect upon a particular community; the effect of its policies on broad issues such as inflation or our relations with Latin America; whether its products are manufactured under sanitary conditions or correctly labeled. Even the good taste of a corporation's advertising or sponsored television shows is called into question, often in a most public fashion. When this criticism comes—and it is part of the daily grist —it is the job of top management of a large corporation to be prepared to defend and justify and explain; to find compromises between conflicting interests of every conceivable kind.

The fact that institutional advertising and public relations expenditures are today well accepted and conventional is one indication of how far we have gone from the days when a company head could snort and say, "The public!—we don't owe the public anything."

Our top industrial leadership has assumed, and it now bears, not only responsibility for production itself, but for a whole range of the social and political problems which are to be found in a modern industrialized nation. In short, there has been a revolution in the nature of active responsibility of Big Business. The president of a large company is now responsible to practically everybody!

It is certainly not true that all, or perhaps even a majority, of the top officers and directors of the five thousand larger corporate enterprises of the country as yet accept or even fully comprehend the idea that broad public accountability is part of the modern responsibility of business. But this is the definite—and inescapable—trend.

This remarkable change in the nature of business responsibility has progressed so far that it has a direct and vital bearing on whether concentration of industry endangers the liberties and fortunes of the American people. To put it another way, the change in public accountability on the part of industrial management is a reflection of the effectiveness of the new checks and balances upon abuses of economic power. It raises sharply the question of how substantial and how relevant today are the traditional and historical fears of Big Business.

3

Big Business for a Big Country

THE people of the United States of America now produce as much as all the rest of the people of the world put together, with a mere 6 per cent of the world's population and about the same per cent of its land area and natural resources. This production will probably be increased greatly in the next ten to twenty-five years. It is only at the beginning.

At this moment this is the most important fact in the world, for it is America's mastery of productivity that stands between freedom and the tidal wave of Communist militarism threatening the world with a new era of darkness.

This technique of production—and with it the equally important art of an ethical distribution of production—is a *creative* thing, a combination of poetry and sweat. It calls for imagination, vitality, faith, as well as the skills of science, management, human relations and modern governmental techniques. This unfolding of American productive and social genius is the most exciting spectacle in the history of modern times.

Man has been working at wealth creation since the beginning of time in order to fight off hunger, exposure, degradation. He has been trying to push back his enemy, poverty, trying for enough breathing space so his whole day and night would not be needed just to get enough food and warmth and shelter to survive. He has been trying to get a margin so he could be a man, not merely an animal fighting to stay alive.

In America of the mid-fifties of this century, we have done this wealth-creation job better by all odds than any generation ever did. Our over-all productivity keeps climbing year after year. Since 1939 we have doubled our total industrial production; and we go right on adding to it year after year.

More important still, we are learning, through an imaginative synthesis of private and governmental action, how to get the benefits of this vast flood of goods and services distributed in a democratic and an ethical way. The result is fewer very poor and fewer very rich than in any large community since the dawn of history.

What accounts for this almost-miracle? It is very important indeed that we try to understand why this great and creative art came to fruition now, in mid-twentieth century U.S.A., and what it is we can do to stimulate and nourish this distinctive talent of ours. I have thought about this a great deal, as have ever so many other people.

Here is a summary of my thinking:

First: Our productive and distributive superiority, our economic fruitfulness, rest upon Bigness. Size is our greatest single functional asset.

Second: Against the dangers of Bigness—concentration of economic power and overcentralization—we either already have adequate public safeguards, or know how to fashion new ones as required.

Third: We need to sense what an asset we have in Bigness. We need to examine it critically, but affirmatively, without old and outworn prejudices.

Fourth: The time has come when it is in the interest of the whole country that we promote and encourage and nourish those principles and practices of Bigness that can bring us, in increasing measure, vast social and individual benefits. We can deliberately and consciously fashion public safeguards and private incentives whereby through Bigness we can bring closer to reality the American dream: individual freedom, social justice, material well-being, world moral leadership.

Our present legal policy concerning Bigness is embodied in a latter-day interpretation of the Sherman and Clayton antitrust laws. Those laws were enacted many years ago as the creative Magna Carta of economic freedom for an America emerging from an agricultural economy. There are few greater legislative achievements than these laws that struck at the monopoly practices of the trusts of the nineties and the early years of this century, with their price agreements, pools, rebates and the ruthless slaughter of industrial newcomers. It is clear that business-policing activities to ferret out and punish specific crimes against competition need to be maintained and even increased in vigor; on this I have further comment at a later point in this book.

But the doctrine that Bigness is an evil, in and of itself, and against the Sherman Act even though there are no specific acts against competition, is a thoroughly unsound development of our governmental policy toward Bigness; it is a policy that cripples our country.

Such an interpretation of the fundamental business laws of the country, and our antagonistic, suspicious emotions toward Bigness are out of tune with the realities of the twentieth-century industrial and urban country we are today. This confusion and conflict prevent the full flowering of the advantages of Bigness so valuable to us, and so greatly needed for our national security. We are dependent upon big-scale undertakings, and not alone of private business, but also co-operatives, nonprofit mutual organizations and governmental institutions. Our urgent need, then, is to recognize the great social asset we have in Bigness.

America is a country with a special talent for Bigness; but by this I do not mean to imply that it is *only* the United States that has shown such talent. The United Kingdom and Canada both contain outstanding examples of Big Business, of course, and so do several European industrial nations. But it is the United States that is most characteristically a country of large-scale undertakings.

I am aware that in advocating better understanding and a more affirmative climate of opinion toward big-scale undertakings I move in a highly controversial field. It is an area where equally sensible and public-spirited men disagree, and where the memory of past corporate wrongs and abuses makes difficult a calm and objective analysis of today's circumstances. But these matters, controversial as they are, need to be discussed in the open air of reason. They need to be discussed widely, on their present merits, with a minimum of emotion, except the dominant emotion of furthering the strength and health of a country hard pressed with the increasing burdens of world leadership.

Some of the issues concerned with Bigness are necessarily discussed by legal and economic experts with such detail and complexity as to be beyond the understanding of most of us. This I have tried to avoid, and in doing so may have laid myself open to the charge that I have oversimplified.

I have not attempted to set up a precise definition of what is "big" in business. When I write of Bigness in industry, however, I do *not* by any means refer only to the relatively few corporations at the very top in size: Du Pont, General Electric, Union Carbide, U. S. Steel, etc. In 1937, the Twentieth Century Fund, in a study entitled "Big Business," described as the "giants" those "with total assets in 1933 of at least $50,000,000 or total net income of at least $5,000,000 each." Today (only twenty years later) we would not, of course, classify corporations no larger than this minimum as the "giants." They would of course qualify as "big" today; yet units half this size or even less in some industries are examples of Big Business. Even what is sometimes called "medium-sized" business is huge by almost any standard. This is a country of Bigness.

The argument about what is big enough and what is too big, I regard, generally, as not the central issue. My concern here is with the establishing to the fullest of a *climate of opportunity for growth and attainment of size,* as a means of greater productivity, better distribution of goods and income, and greater well-being for the country.

I have tried to avoid reopening what I regard as a sterile quarrel between "little business" and "Big Business," as if we were faced with a choice of one or the other. That we need "little business" is too clear to require argument, and that smaller business has not been extinguished by Bigness is manifest. There are—outside of agriculture—more than 4,000,000 firms in this country, and 40 per cent of total private national income is produced by unincorporated business proprietors. More than one-third of the country's output (aside from farming) is produced by what the census classifies as "small business"; and more than half the corporate assets of the country are owned by 500,000 small or medium-sized corporations.

What is more important than such figures is to comprehend that it is of the essence of Bigness that it *creates diversity* in size of business, big *and* little—and nourishes diversity: diversity of size and of function, so that what is small becomes bigger, so that what is big in turn creates many little businesses, which in turn compete with and stimulate and discipline what is big. Of this mutually invigorating relation between big and small business I shall have more to say in later chapters.

Nor am I here concerned with economic prejudice, inflamed by dated oratorical flourishes and trumpetings that our fate is controlled by a "handful of rich and all-powerful men." This is a picture faded, unreal, a quaint daguerreotype of a world that is no more.

"As I belong to the class of people who have great faith in this country," wrote Henry Adams to his friend Charles Milnes Gaskell in 1877, "and who believe that in another century it will be saying, in its turn, the last word of civilization, I enjoy the expectation of the coming day. . . ."*

I, too, "enjoy the expectation of the coming day." But whether such faith is sustained by the event depends upon the answer to this question: As a people, will we be *big* enough? We have indeed climbed to new heights in human history, we Americans of the mid-twentieth century. Now what? Will we lose our great chance because we do not ourselves understand and therefore cannot fully use one of the vital secrets of our own strength?

An individual cannot do his best if he is confused about basic things. Neither can a nation. This nation *is* confused, for we say one thing about size in business, and we do another and almost opposite thing. We distrust and inhibit and even threaten with criminal proceedings the very economic talent which is one of our sources of strength and freedom, our capacity for large-scale undertakings.

Our basic economic law, the Sherman Antitrust Act, as it is more recently construed, symbolizes our distrust, giving concrete expression to a temperamental aver-

* *The Selected Letters of Henry Adams,* ed. by Newton Arvin. Farrar, Strauss and Young, Inc., 1951, xxvi.

sion to Bigness and to our belief in competition. How sometimes confused and contradictory this idea is I shall demonstrate in a later chapter by indicating that today Bigness in industry is itself one of the most effective ways— sometimes the only effective way—to maintain genuine competition.

The belief that Bigness is, in itself, something evil is a theme that runs through the political thinking of this country. The same theme, with only minor variations, has been repeated in the political campaigns of both Republicans and Democrats. Usually described as "concentration of economic power," the ever-mounting size of corporate undertakings has been, and continues to this day to be, the subject of unremitting criticism, suspicion, warning, attack and governmental action.

At the time the Federal Trade Commission was established in 1914, a Joint Committee told Congress: "The concentration of wealth, money, and property in the United States under the control and in the hands of a few individuals or great corporations has grown to such an enormous extent that unless checked it will ultimately threaten the perpetuity of our institutions."

Nearly forty years later, in 1951, the Federal Trade Commission used almost the same words: "If nothing is done to check the growth in concentration, either the giant corporations will ultimately take over the country, or the government will be impelled to step in and impose some form of direct regulation."

We Americans are individualists. This is one of our great and distinctive qualities. Our whole philosophy and outlook are built around the individual, the smallest unit of all. This individualism runs through everything we do. We reject the idea of being cogs in a big machine.

So, being individualists, it is not unnatural that initially we should distrust Bigness. Most of us, brought up on trust busting and the fear of monopoly, have imbedded in our memory the history of abuses, arrogance and disregard of public and individual welfare by large-scale business in past decades.

We do not as yet fully comprehend what profound changes have taken place in the past three decades, or that our dependence is today upon Bigness for the very security of the country.

It is big enterprise that provides the American people with many of the things we want. The things we want are not only physical things—goods and services, the "highest standard of living in the world." Size accounts in a measure for those things we want which are *not* physical and material, but without which we could not enjoy such physical things as shelter, food, clothing, recreation.

So that when I speak of Bigness I am not thinking simply of "efficiency" of large-scale production and distribution. I am thinking of people, about my friends and neighbors and their aspirations and hopes and needs as individuals. To a large degree our human needs, our nonmaterial needs, are determined by the physical setting of our lives, by how we as a people earn our living, produce and distribute goods and services, how we build and manage our communities. The prospect of maintaining those human values we hold dear, our standards of what is good and what is

shoddy or evil, depends largely upon this physical setting
we usually call our economic system. I am not myself so
much interested in the system as such, as in its purposes
and its consequences for individual values and standards.

I conceive the purpose of American economic society
not as the production and consumption of so many billions
of units of steel, copper, automobiles, refrigerators. The
purpose of our economic society and system is to promote
freedom for the individual, as one prime essential of happi-
ness and human fulfillment. By freedom I mean essentially
freedom to choose to the maximum degree possible. Freedom is by no means merely a freedom to vote without coercion. "Did you suppose," asked Walt Whitman, "democracy was only for elections, for politics?"

Freedom of choice in economic matters means freedom
to choose between competing ideas or services or goods. It
means the maximum freedom to choose one job or one pro-
fession or one line of business as against some other. It
means a maximum range of choice for the consumer when
he spends his dollar. It means a maximum possible area of
choice for the man who has saved up capital to invest.

These are economic choices. They are, however, more
than economic or business acts. They are the mark of men
who are free, as free as in society it is possible or workable
for men to be. We call our economic system, quite appropriately, free enterprise. To maintain and nourish the
essentials of free enterprise for all our people we must
maintain and nourish the freedom of choice that makes
the system come into being and flourish.

It is the vital role of Big Business in furthering just this freedom of choice that I emphasize in this book. And yet we still carry around our inherited conviction that Bigness means monopoly, which implics the absence of free choice.

It is natural enough that we should so generally regard *Bigness* and *monopoly* as synonymous. During the first years of this century, when many of us acquired our economic and political ideas, it was so often the case that Bigness and monopoly tended to be the same.

There were periodic curbs put on Big Business through these years. Woodrow Wilson created the Federal Trade Commission. Charles Evans Hughes, writing a great chapter of devoted public service, exposed the evils of big utilities and insurance companies. Louis D. Brandeis, with the power of his great spirit and mind, exposed the "curse of bigness," and it was anything but a pretty picture.

The depression of the thirties brought a resurgence of public condemnation and distrust of size: the Pecora investigation of Wall Street, the Temporary Economic Committee, the constructive and overdue reforms of the abuses of finance and large business during the first seven years of the administrations of Franklin Roosevelt.

The apparent contradictions of my own experience are illustrative of those of almost everyone else. I was brought up, like most men and women of my generation, to be suspicious and distrustful of things that are big. My father and his friends, who were small businessmen, spoke with deep apprehension of the trusts and cheered Teddy Roosevelt in his Bull Moose campaign; they thought the world was in a bad way when the first five-and-ten bought out an old individual family business and began the "chain-store" influx in our Indiana town. At home and at school, my generation heard the same refrain of fear and antagonism and distrust of Bigness—though at the same time we bragged about things because they were big. And yet by the time I was forty, I found myself directing the biggest integrated power system in the world, the TVA, which was itself the creation of an old-time trust buster, George Norris, and an outstanding critic of Bigness, Franklin D. Roosevelt. For over thirteen years I helped develop, as a unit, a region larger geographically than Great Britain, that embraced parts of seven Southern states. And, in 1946, I was made head of the largest industrial monopoly of history, the Atomic Energy Commission of the United States.

Despite our antagonism, despite handicaps of law and public opinion, Bigness of units has nevertheless developed rapidly until today size is a chief and outstanding characteristic of the way we do business, the way we live. And we like the material fruits of size at the very same time that we continue to view it with distrust. There is an apparent contradiction between our deep fears of Bigness and our need of it, that for a good many years has confused and troubled me. Can these two be reconciled? More narrowly, can Bigness and competition be reconciled?

The Sherman Antitrust Act has had a profound effect upon the course of American economic and social development. It was a great feat of statesmanship, an exhibition of remarkable insight.

But to the extent that it has recently been so construed as to condemn Bigness *per se,* the Sherman Act does not live up to the present needs of the United States. For basic reasons going to the very dynamics of modern industry, it is Bigness that helps keep competition a flourishing reality today, a subject fully discussed in Part III.

It is not, however, with the provisions and interpretations of the Sherman Act that we laymen should be deeply concerned today, but with the underlying assumptions, "the picture in the mind," the philosophy for which that act stands as it is applied to large-scale undertakings. It is the economic and political philosophy and emotion, affecting its present interpretation, that badly needs re-examination. It is by the new facts of the fifties in contrast to the essential facts about our country as it was a generation or two ago, that we need to judge whether Bigness should today be penalized or encouraged, feared or promoted.

Such a fundamental re-examination is appropriate, is indeed essential and vital, at a time like the present. In such a period of crisis and strain, of heart-searching and anxiety about basic things, we need to examine such an all-pervasive issue as this. If, by that inexplicable process of general public consensus by which Americans determine fundamental issues, we decide that Bigness is our ally, that its risk and dangers are now manageable and with wisdom can be surmounted, if we conclude to end this contradiction between our enjoyment of the fruits of Bigness and the suspicions we visit on it, then we can accelerate our progress toward the goals of America in a way that takes one's breath away to contemplate.

PART II

BIGNESS AND THE NEW COMPETITION

4

Bigness—the Life of Trade

COMPETITION, always the mainspring of our economy and of the dynamics of American life, in mid-twentieth century America has been stimulated and quickened by Big Business. As a consequence competition has taken on a renewed vitality and diversity, a new dimension and a new content. Indeed, we are living in what is probably the most highly competitive society men have ever known.

This New Competition provides for the individual American an enriched variety, breadth and freedom of choice. There is today, for a large proportion of the citizenry, a wider scope for the exercise of individual tastes and desires than has ever existed in any other civilization.

Moreover, Big Business, with its mounting emphasis upon research, has increased the freedom of business newcomers to enter many industries in competition with the existing long-established firms. This significant development, commonly referred to in business circles as "diversification," constitutes a creative broadening of competition and thereby of business and individual opportunity.

This increased tempo of competition, paced by Big Business, has not made small business extinct, as has been predicted from time to time; there has indeed been a contrary effect for efficient, enterprising and imaginative smaller business. The modern function of Big Business and big research has provided for these a kind of opportunity that did not previously exist, not only for the creation of new independent business, but also for the proliferation and growth of small and medium business into Big Business.

Moreover, this New Competition has promoted rather than inhibited a diversity in the various *forms* of large economic enterprise, as the flourishing state of business cooperatives and nonprofit mutual associations testifies.

Most important of all, to my way of thinking, latter-day competition has given a zest and sparkle and a dynamic fluid quality to the economic life of America. This in turn has spurred social change, and stimulated the imagination of the country as to its latent powers of creativeness in every field, not only economic but political and civic and cultural. It has made this country, more than ever before, a young people's country.

The New Competition, as a consequence of its faith in research and development, has heightened the prestige of research, and therefore the standing in the community of the kind of men who excel in this intellectual area. This has had the effect, among other things, of increasing respect for learning and thinking, and of furthering "the idea of progress," an article of faith that is a basic tenet of our liberal democratic philosophy.

These comments on the health of competition in the United States are, I believe, readily confirmed by everyday observation. I shall refer to a good deal of such supporting evidence later in this and succeeding chapters.

Why, then, have those whose responsibility it has been to safeguard competition, such as the lawyers and economists of the Department of Justice and the Federal Trade Commission, been so professionally gloomy, in season and out, about the state of competition? Why is it that Congressional committees dealing with small business or monopoly, on which sit some able and conscientious Representatives and Senators, take such a dim view of Bigness, decry the asserted "alarming increase in concentration of economic power" and blame Bigness for a trend away from competition? When the facts are so readily available, the proof of good results so evident, why is it that only rarely does one hear a public servant or a responsible candidate for office of either party, or an independent and respected publicist speak out realistically on this subject?

"Politics" is sometimes ascribed as the reason. But this does not explain why public opinion apparently makes it good politics to take a view so contrary to experience and everyday observation.

One underlying explanation, it occurs to me, may be this: Many of those whose views influence public opinion indict Big Business as a threat to competition because they have a wholly different concept of *what constitutes competition* than the facts of life in mid-century U.S.A. warrant. In short, they are preoccupied with the old, not the new, competition.

This older picture of competition, in general, is that of

38364

many small competitors. Even so great a judge as Learned Hand seems to accept the assumption that there can be no other kind.

"Throughout the history of these [antitrust] statutes," he held, in an opinion as recent as 1945, "it has been constantly assumed that one of their purposes was to perpetuate and preserve, for its own sake and in spite of possible cost, an organization of industry in small units which can effectively compete with each other."*

According to this concept, for each of these many competitors market processes determine his costs pretty largely, such costs as labor, transportation, fuel, energy, etc. Each of these elements of cost—labor, fuel, etc.—is arrived at, in turn, as a consequence of the competition of many small units. Competition, according to this picture, forces the lowest costs; the "marginal firm" falls overboard; the result is the lowest prices for the consumer. Thus is the individual protected, as consumer and as citizen, by automatic economic forces, against large aggregations of capital or labor able to control costs or impose its will.

In this older but still popular notion of competition, *price* is the major issue in the contest for business. The existence or nonexistence of price differences virtually concludes the issue of whether or not competition exists. If prices do not vary, it must be "presumed" that a conspiracy among competitors not to compete exists. Finally, this older competition, essentially a nineteenth-century picture, is thought of chiefly as one between producers or distributors of the *same* product—*between* producers of lumber, steel, wool, cotton textiles and so on.

* U.S. v. Aluminum Co. of America 148 F. 2d 416,429 (1945).

We are told—in party platforms, judicial opinions and Senate reports—that only as we are able to bring back *this* kind of competition can free competitive enterprise survive.

It is hardly necessary to point out to any observant adult today what a dream world this older picture of competition conjures up. In the first place, any notion that most producers or manufacturers today control or can unilaterally determine some of the largest elements of their costs is palpable nonsense. Labor costs, often the bulk of manufacturing costs today, are as a rule determined by agreements with unions. In most industries the labor rates are on a nationwide basis, that is, for all competitors as a class. Rail transportation rates on raw materials, finished products, fuel, etc., are fixed by law on a regional or nationwide basis. The rates for electrical energy or gas and therefore their cost are fixed by law. Social security costs are fixed by law for all competitors, as are the rates of excise and sales taxes. Federal income tax, the largest factor in business computations, is not ordinarily regarded as a "cost," but as a major expense it is certainly a fact that affects competition in a profound way; income tax rates are of course standard for all who compete.

This partial enumeration does not mean that there is not still a very great deal of room for ingenuity and skill as between competitors. But it does mean that the crucial battleground of competition as to costs has shifted to new terrain, to the fields of improvement in management techniques (which usually require Bigness), to better personnel practices (where Bigness has excelled compared with small units), and to new technological developments (which usually require size).

Similarly old-fashioned and incongruous is the orthodox preoccupation with price competition as the touchstone of the existence or nonexistence of competition.

In the first place, with the larger components of most costs predetermined for all competitors, often at the very same rates—labor, transportation, energy, employee welfare, taxes—major cost variations and therefore wide price disparities for identical products would be surprising. But quite aside from this situation, the fact, as every layman knows, is that price today is by no means the determining element of business rivalry and of consumer preference. In the field of industrial purchasing particularly, competition more often than not centers on peculiar suitability to the user's needs (which producers have studied in detail) on engineering design, durability, low operating and maintenance cost, and scores of other similar considerations usually of more importance to the user's costs than purchase price. Much the same considerations now apply to consumer goods, in which superior packaging, style, color, flavor, durability, weigh heavily in the mind of the customers. It is here that advertising has served such a useful economic function.

Perhaps in a completely rational (though rather dull) world these "features" of styling, color, etc., of which so much is made in competitive selling would be eliminated, with price of standardized items the sole criterion of choice. But fortunately for the fun of living, we continue to be a highly individual people. We like to be appealed to on the basis of our differing likes and tastes and opinions. The great mail-order merchandisers, which once concentrated almost exclusively for their appeal on lowest price, have realized this strong American trait. One can see this graphically by leafing through their catalogues, comparing the styling and number of items carried today as against twenty years ago. Henry Ford the elder nearly lost in a competitive race in which he had a long lead because he insisted that price, not style and color and doodads, was what people wanted in a car: "You can have any color Ford you want as long as it is black!"

The tenet of the orthodox dogma that competition only thrives when there are *many* and relatively small producers is similarly out of date and largely unrealistic. Today a large proportion of our production in basic industries comes from a relatively few very large concerns. Since this is a departure from the nineteenth-century ideal of a competitive system, adherents of this older concept continue today, as they have for a generation, to seek to break up large production or distribution entities into many smaller ones, and to prevent smaller ones from merging. By this process of dismemberment or inhibition on growth they seek to restore to life an inferior and superseded kind of competitive society. The fact that under our present Big Business economy competition of the liveliest kind exists *in fact*, as any consumer or industrialist knows, is simply ignored, or is deemed irrelevant since it is not the *kind* of competition that fits the older picture.

Indeed, some economic scholars became so committed to a theoretical and abstract picture of what competition is that they have invented new words to describe the competitive relations in an industry of Big Business, calling it not simply a form of competition but "oligopoly." The meaning is probably plain to economists; but to the ordinary man this term sounds like a peculiarly repulsive form of monopoly; it has the same general effect on the hearer as was intended by the candidate on the stump who charged his opponent with "committing nepotism with his sister-in-law."

Now "competition" is a fine sturdy old word. It does have a special and scholarly meaning to economists, one that is wholly justified for their analytic and teaching needs. But it is not exclusively a technical term for experts' use only. To most of us laymen, competition means struggle, contest, rivalry, matching of wits or strength. Competition is something that keeps you on your toes. It is a spirit of living, a spirit highly developed and greatly enjoyed in this country, whether the "competition" is between Republicans and Democrats, Yankees and Dodgers, television and movies, between classical music and bebop, Esso gasoline and Texaco, between objective art and abstract art, between the independent grocer and the Safeway store, between ideas of how the country should be run, or differing beliefs as to the nature of the good life.

To the noneconomist, competition *in business* is but one manifestation of this spirit of conflict and rivalry of ideas. It describes the effort to persuade the customer that you have made a better mousetrap, or perhaps that if he buys your product he won't need a mousetrap. Competition in business is the spirit of finding *a better way of doing what people want done* or that you can persuade them they want done. Whatever tends to keep the contest of skill and wits and strength and ingenuity lively is part of competition.

Why fuss with the way economists use the word "competition?" What difference does it make, as a practical matter, what competition is called? It makes a great deal of difference, in my opinion.

One reason the very existence of Bigness is so often assumed to be monopolistic is the use the scholarly economist makes of the term "competition" in teaching and writing, to express an abstract concept of competition of many small units. This conceptual use of the term, and the invention by economists of other and distinguishing terms such as oligopoly, duopoly, imperfect competition, monopolistic competition, countervailing power, etc., has tended to obscure the fact that rivalry between a few big units is definitely competition. Thus a popular misuse of a theoretician's term has led to unsound public policy and confused thinking by laymen—in short, has been injurious to the public interest.

No one should object to economists being economists, and using the technical tools of their calling. If a theoretical concept of competition is a useful device for their scholarly or pedagogical purposes, they certainly cannot be criticized for using it.

But it is a matter of concern when the economists' analytical device leads judges, trust busters, and legislators to interpret theories as if they were facts, as a condition that actually exists or could exist, when it should be plain that it doesn't, and couldn't, and shouldn't.

From this confusion between a scholarly concept and the facts of life practical consequences follow. Thus, the conclusion in the courts and in public opinion that Bigness and monopoly are more or less synonymous; or the conclusion that if in an industry there are big units, few in number, these Big Businesses, *by definition* and quite aside from any specific course of conduct, impair rather than promote competition.

Economists cannot wholly absolve themselves from some responsibility for the popular interpretations—or misinterpretations—of what some of them for a generation have taught, as theory, to thousands in their classes. Many of these students now occupy positions where college-bred misimpressions and confusions between fact and abstraction can and often are hurtful to us all. Good teaching and scholarly leadership in the social sciences requires that economists accept a measure of responsibility—as the best among them have—to see to it that their students (especially those whose training in economics stops with elementary courses) and the public generally are able to distinguish between what is taught and used as a theoretical device, and what is operating fact.

The New Competition appears in a variety of forms, and has many distinctive characteristics. The balance of Part II is devoted largely to a description and to illustrations of a few of these, for the purpose of pointing up the central place of Bigness in creating these latter-day types of competition.

Among the principal kinds, characteristics and qualities

of modern competition are the following upon which I shall comment in the succeeding chapters.

1. Competition between alternatives, the essence of which is summarized in these words of Mr. Justice Holmes: ". . . thus the final competition is between the objects of desire, and therefore between the producers of those objects." This may assume many forms, such as the substitution of one product for another, the creation of entirely new products for newly found needs, the adaptation of an existing product for a new use, and so on.

2. Major reliance upon research, principally for the discovery and development of new or improved products, but also for marketing, management improvement, etc., as a major tenet of competition.

3. Entry of newcomers into an established area of industry, to compete for a share of that business, often called "diversification"; or to compete indirectly by producing their own needs which previously had been produced by the established industry, or to perform for themselves services or operations previously supplied by the established firms—a form of expansion ordinarily known as "industrial integration."

4. Increasing the geographic area of competition—"One Big Market."

5. Competition within a single organization, *between* its departments or subsidiaries and affiliates, between the various products of the same concern, or between different functions (e.g., engineers and salesmen) within the same concern.

6. Advertising as an integral and major function of competition.

5

Competition—Between the "Objects of Desire"

THE heart of the New Competition is competition between different ways of meeting the same or a similar need or demand for goods or services. An incident out of my experience in the running of a public business, the TVA, illustrates this thesis.

In order to interconnect the existing dam at Muscle Shoals with the whole series of new dams that, in 1933, TVA began to build on the Tennessee River, it was necessary to erect thousands of miles of new high-tension electric lines. Copper was the customary material for transmission lines of such high voltage. TVA needed huge amounts for this new network. At that time the copper mining and fabricating industry was in the doldrums. Mines were closed, smelters and refineries were running only part time, stocks of unsold copper were piled high.

But when TVA went into the market to buy copper transmission lines, the cost seemed excessive, with prices identical, or nearly identical, no matter what producer we turned to. Whether this meant that there was collusion between copper producers and fabricators rather than competition within the industry, we did not know. But it would not help to request the Department of Justice to institute antitrust proceedings on that assumption. To win an antitrust suit after five or more years of litigation would not provide transmission lines at once, which was what was needed.

We had an alternative, and an attractive one, as it turned out, namely to build these transmission lines of aluminum. There would be dollar savings running into large figures. There would also, it developed, be significant operating advantages in aluminum conductors over those made of copper. Accordingly, we decided to build the transmission lines of the Tennessee Valley of aluminum.

The huge Aluminum Company of America was, at that time, the only producer of virgin aluminum in the country. As such it was usually referred to as monopolistic. But it was this monopoly—in the sense of a *sole* producer—that provided the means by which the benefits of a competitive system were made a reality, in this important instance. Moreover, this competition between two different ways of transmitting electricity gave the Aluminum Company an added financial incentive for research to improve further its product so it could capture more and more of this transmission-line market, as it has done. As a significant side light, the most recent company to enter the field of primary aluminum production—in 1952—is one of the great producers of copper, the Anaconda Copper Company. Competition between alternatives—copper and aluminum—has spurred both industries.

Here was a case of genuine and effective competition, a real choice for the consumer, with the stimulating effects on industry that bona fide competition is intended to bring. There was no visible competition between copper producers, nor between aluminum producers (there being only one of the latter at the time), yet there was real protection to the consumer and genuine activation of the spirit of enterprise from the competition between two different materials.

I am not saying that active competition between the producers of the same product is of no present consequence. It certainly is. My point is that under present-day conditions it is often the least significant form. The competition between alternative materials, or ways of satisfying human needs and desires, has become a new dimension of competition. Here is the real battleground in the fight to keep competitive conditions that will yield the greatest benefits to society and to the individual.

To the extent that we increase man's opportunity for selection and choice, to that extent we have nourished and strengthened real competition. This is the core of the New Competition. One of the greatest differences between economic conditions of today and those that prevailed when our ideas about Bigness and monopoly were in formation lies in this widening of free choice for the individual or business enterprise.

Take another familiar illustration: fuel. There was a time not too long ago when coal was our only basic fuel. Competition in fuel was virtually synonymous with competition among coal producers. If a few companies got control of coal production and eliminated competition by agreement, such chief coal users as the power companies would have had no alternative but to pay the prices demanded; and the householder would either pay or shiver.

Today coal is still a vital fuel, but it is no longer the only fuel. Oil has taken the place of coal on many railroads. Coal has left the kitchen in favor of gas and electricity. Oil, gas and even electricity now heat millions of homes and factories once dependent entirely upon coal. This new kind of competition has provided a spur for the coal industry. It has brought benefits for its customers. It has been largely responsible for bigger coal companies, by growth and merger. In these larger companies there are improved management, increased mechanization of coal mining, and the highest standards of productivity, safety and human welfare in the long history of this industry.

Cotton once was "king," and there really was no substitute for wool. If you wanted fabrics and textiles you made them of cotton or wool, or you went without. (Silk and linen were not really important.) Almost all clothing and textiles and fabrics for the home came from one or both of these staples. Within the cotton and wool industries there was a highly competitive field, both in the raising of the raw material and in its fabrication.

Cotton and wool producers today, however, must compete not only among themselves but with a whole series of new man-made fibers that find their way into men's suits and women's dresses, into rugs and draperies and blankets, into electric insulation and tire cord, into ropes and sails and socks. Some of these are "true synthetics," derived from gas and other chemicals; some are fibers made of wood pulp and the like.

Whereas synthetics a few years ago competed only with cotton and wool, today they compete furiously among themselves as well, for their variety is already very great. There is rayon, the elder brother, and acetate, both made from wood pulp and cotton linters. There is vicara from corn protein, and glass fiber from sand and limestone. From chemicals derived largely from petroleum or natural gas come nylon, dacron, acrilan, orlon, x-51, dynel and others, with still others on the way.

Today a "conspiracy" to fix the price or limit the output of cotton or wool would be undesirable in theory and certainly contrary to the Sherman Antitrust Law, but its effect on consumers would be largely irrelevant. A new kind of competition unknown to Senator Sherman and Teddy Roosevelt and the trust busters has come into being, and has given a new vitality and broader meaning to competition and thereby to the health of the American economy.

Not the least reassuring aspect of this kind of keen competitive struggle between different ways of meeting the same need—or creating a new need—is the element of broad adjustment and flexibility inherent in the process. True, the automobile did not "supplement" the horse and buggy; it put them completely out of business. There are other comparable instances. But the more common situation is this: the new way and the old way supplement and complement each other. By some ingenious combination or interdevelopment *both* continue to be used, or put together they add up to something wholly new. Thus, when radio first appeared, a newcomer and a competitor of wire communication, the A. T. & T. saw in it, as General David Sarnoff pointed out twenty-five years ago, "the invisible connecting link that would make telephony possible across the seas, and thus gave the world its first commercial transatlantic telephone service. In [radio] broadcasting it joined wires and wireless into a complete communication unit and thus contributed much to the upbuilding of the broadcasting art."

Often the new entry, far from replacing the older contestant for public favor, stimulates the total demand so there is greater use of both old and new. A familiar case is the coming of radio into the home. The phonograph people feared this new "music box" would put records out of business. The very opposite has happened, of course. In volume and variety the phonograph and recording business has never been so flourishing. In fact the phonograph and the radio, which was going to "ruin" it, are customarily found cozily together in the same living-room instrument, and now not infrequently nesting together with still another "alternative" to both radio and phonograph, television.

The contest between cotton and wool and synthetic fibers may turn out to yield a comparable result—a mixture of both materials in such satisfactory combinations as to increase total wool and cotton sales beyond what they ever reached when they had the whole market to themselves. Nothing better illustrates, to my mind, the richly creative, diverse and undogmatic nature of American industry today than this quality of adaptation to the new.

Another vital area of our economic life—transportation —provides still another illustration of the competition of alternatives. Much of the antagonism to Big Business had its origin in the days when railroads were the only means of mass transport. The building of the transcontinental railroads was a feat of imagination and daring, without which the country could not have developed as it did in the post-Civil War period. But, in keeping with the standards of the day, there were many abuses. Thus the Midwest farmer, wanting to ship to Chicago from the local elevator, found that he had to use the railroads on the railroads' own terms or let his grain rot.

Some of the greatest lawsuits under the Sherman Act in the earliest days were directed against railroads. Railroad regulation, by the Interstate Commerce Commission and state commissions, was the direct result of public resentment against abuse of power by the railroads.

How well railroad regulation has worked out in practice is a matter on which people disagree. Certainly it is clear that the new form of competition—that of a choice between alternative means—has completely changed the picture of mass transport.

The truck, the automobile and the bus, the airplane and the re-emergence of river freight traffic, all combine to provide very active competition in transportation service. We have become the most mobile large nation on earth.

Could antitrust suits or regulation of the railroads alone

have done for American transport what this multiplication of the means of transport has accomplished? Whatever the answer to this question, certainly the issue in railroad regulation these days no longer centers (as it did when I first came to the bar in 1923) about the legal or constitutional right of the railroad to a certain return on its value or investment. The issue now, in most freight cases, is what rate—or improved quality of service—will meet the competition of some other available form of transportation.

In almost every aspect of our life the New Competition is providing us with a kind of "competition . . . between the objects of desire" undreamed of in the days of the trust busters.

Thus glass—the most ancient of industrial products— is no longer "just glass." Because of extensive research and development, glass now competes actively as a fabric for many uses; as a building and insulation material it competes with concrete and brick and asbestos. Glass, in its turn, faces new competition in its most familiar role, as a bottle: the coated-paper milk "bottle," the "tin" beer can, and the plastic bottle, for examples. But paper as a packaging material now must compete with chemicals drawn from coal, for phenolic resin, made into an almost weightless foam, is edging into the field of featherweight shipping materials. One of the oldest strongholds of metal —the iron and copper pipe—is now meeting spirited competition, for special uses, from plastic pipe.

Radio competes with the transatlantic cable; the microwave relay competes with the telephone and telegraph. Sawdust, the soybean, the cornstalk and cob compete with petroleum and steel and wood and copper as industrial raw materials for plastics, textiles, chemicals.

The technical achievement of television contends for public favor with motion pictures, providing the public with more honest-to-goodness competition and improvement in the motion-picture industry than all the numerous antitrust proceedings involving the movies put together. The process goes on steadily, each week bringing some new technical advance that in turn widens the spectrum of choice. This competition, more lively and constructive than has ever been seen before, is the consequence of technology, not of policing activities of government.

One of the most important manifestations of the competition of alternatives is that between man power and machine power.

Although it is a political and ethical fundamental with us that the labor of human beings is not a commodity, nevertheless in an economic sense labor does compete *with* a commodity, to wit machines. With the oncoming of technology the balance always has to be struck between the cost and effectiveness of doing a job entirely with the energy of men, or partly with man power and partly with machines, or (more recently) almost entirely by machines, with no human intervention for hours at a time.

There was a time in recent social history when it was thought to be in the humane spirit to view with repugnance this economic or cost competition between men and these inanimate "monsters." The term "robot" came into the vernacular, accompanied by a flood of feeling that machines were the enemies of the finer side of human life.

American big industry, with the co-operation of most organized labor, has pretty well demonstrated that the result of this competition between men and their machines has been not only greater productivity and wider distribution of the products thereof, but actually it can be the beginning of a new era of humaneness. Only one who has never spent week after weary week working with a shovel and wheelbarrow or axe and two-man saw, can be aroused by the inhumanity of the bulldozer and the mechanized saw. Here again, the competition of alternatives has paid off, the competition not of one man against another man, but of man's back competing with man's intelligence, as embodied in machinery.

What may well prove the most revolutionary of all such competitive balances is not far off. I have in mind the impending perfection of electronic clerical machines—one might more appropriately call them business-management machines—of a comprehensiveness beyond anything yet available. These will permit the release for more interesting and productive work of a large proportion of the millions of men and women now doing the mountainous record-keeping, the inventory control and procurement paper-work, the bill-writing and the endless fact-reporting tasks required to run our huge insurance, utility, merchandising, postal and other industries, and for the armed forces and other governmental services.

The implications of electronic systems of such scope and flexibility as these upon the very nature and content of the art of management itself, will, in my opinion, be far-reaching.

6

Modern Research and Competition

THE New Competition can be traced to a number of factors, but the central one is the amazing technical advance in American industry due to scientific research and engineering development. The last decade's achievements of the chemical industry and in electronics are perhaps the most spectacular illustrations of how science and technology have intensified competition, and thereby increased the range of free choice that men now have, as contrasted with thirty to fifty years ago. The same thing applies, however, to many other industries.

Great scientific investigations are still sometimes carried out in small laboratories, by one or a few men. But certainly to translate these discoveries into industrial realities is a function of size, except in the most unusual circumstances.

In the 1950 annual report of the country's largest coal company, Pittsburgh Consolidation Coal Company, formed in 1945 by the putting together of some eight smaller companies, there appears this statement as a preface to the report on the company's research program:

One of the stated purposes of the company was to carry on research to find new uses for coal and extend present markets. When this company was formed several years ago no individual coal company was carrying on such a program of any consequence, probably because the industry is made up of so many small units that the cost would have been prohibitive.

It is possible for a whole industry of small units to pool resources and employ private industrial research institutes or universities to carry on particular development work for them. These are usually useful and productive expedients; but they are inferior substitutes, as a general rule, for research and development carried on in a company's own facilities and under its sustained and individual management.

Most significant research and development require large resources and often a long period of time during which no results are forthcoming. The sums of money that have been spent on the development of the Diesel engine, for example, or the gas turbine, are huge. The Diesel development proceeded for more than thirty years before anything commercial resulted. Du Pont spent $27,000,000 over a thirteen-year period before a bolt of nylon could be sold. Krilium, the remarkable chemical substance for changing soil structure, recently announced by Monsanto Chemical Company, is the product of eleven years of research.

The most effective way to "suppress" new inventions or technical ideas is simply not to develop them. Only large enterprises are able to sink the formidable sums of money required to develop basic new departures; a small corporation is rarely able to risk those large sums, perhaps enough to wreck the company if the gamble fails, on the success or failure of a major new project in such areas as electronics or chemicals, for example. Out of a score of promising areas for exploration and exploitation, perhaps only two or three may ever see the light of day as commercial propositions. A pilot plant may cost millions of dollars, take years to build, to be followed perhaps by a costly semi-works plant, and then the results may prove unsatisfactory.

The research work of Big Business multiplies opportunities for smaller businesses, in many areas of American industry, creating the very basis without which hundreds of smaller competitors of Big Business would never come into being, and without which they could not prosper. The already huge television industry, with its array of different manufacturers of all corporate sizes from large to small, came into being only because of persistent and costly research by a few very large concerns.

Equally important, the money and the energy essential to creation of a *demand* for a new product come chiefly from large undertakings, with benefit to small business as well as large—and a resulting general stimulation of competition.

When the Sherman Act set out to protect competition, in 1890, research was almost unknown in American industry. Even in the days of Teddy Roosevelt and the early battles with the trusts there was a total of only 4,000 scientists, of all kinds, in the whole country. The first modern industrial laboratory—General Electric—was not founded until 1900, its staff consisting of two men. Today there are 2,800 such industrial laboratories, manned by 70,000 technical people. "Even thirty years ago," President Conant reminded us recently (1952), "fewer than 20,000 people were employed in all research laboratories of the nation; today the figure is over 250,000."

In 1900 our national expenditure for research was almost nil, and even by 1920 it was only about $60,000,000. Today it is well over $3,000,000,000. The overwhelming proportion—probably in excess of 80 per cent—of this vast research activity is in large undertakings.

The research and development activities carried on by technical agencies of the Federal government demonstrate further how essential Bigness is for modern research— Bigness of pocketbook and of staff.

Some of the ablest scientists and engineers in the world are to be found in the Federal government. For the most part—the needs of military security being the chief exception—their results have been made available to the scientific and technical world and to private industry, with great benefits to all of us, ranging all the way from better phosphatic fertilizers to a clearer understanding of the neutron.

In contrast to this policy of diffusion of technical advance is government secrecy respecting the industrial side of atomic energy. In my opinion, the extremes to which this has been carried has cost and will cost this country heavily in slowing down our industrial progress in the use of a whole new world of peaceful knowledge. A uranium curtain of government monopoly of technical knowledge separates tens of thousands of the ablest minds in industry from the information, the materials and the experience which might benefit us all. The dissemination of this knowledge would not provide the Russians anything they did not steal during the war, or discover for themselves, since it now appears that the Army's "secret" Manhattan Project was a secret only to the American people. This government monopoly over technical thinking, as contrasted with competitive thinking, represents a major departure from all of our paths of industrial progress.*

Government research projects of all kinds, like those of industry, are usually carried on by large enterprises. Even a single technical development of the Bureau of Mines, for example, or the TVA, or the National Advisory Committee for Aeronautics, or the Atomic Energy Commission, sometimes runs into millions of dollars, and requires hundreds of men and vast equipment. In short, Bigness and research activity are largely synonymous whether in business or in government.

The greatest single factor in competition today is indeed research and development. This fact alone makes obsolete and inadequate many of our "horse-and-buggy" ideas about how competition can be maintained.

* The author's views and recommendations in this matter are set out in two articles in *Collier's* Magazine, under the titles "Free the Atom" (June 17, 1950, p. 13) and "Toward the Industrial Atomic Future" (July 15, 1950, p. 14).

7

Competition through Diversification

I N STILL another way Bigness is changing the face of
things in America and profoundly changing the nature
of competition. I refer to the great sweep toward *diversification* in industry of which I have earlier made mention.
The average citizen is hardly aware that this powerful
trend exists, much less that it has attained such giant
proportions in a relatively few years' time.

Few developments in the past twenty-five years hold
such promise for a strengthening of genuine and creative
competition in America.

"Diversified" farming is a well-known idea. When
weather and market conditions are exceptionally good, a
farmer who owns a 400-acre farm, all of it used to raise
corn, or perhaps cotton, benefits by this specialization.
But when things go wrong, he is in a bad way. So he
decides to "diversify." Part of his acreage stays in his staple
cash crop; part of his land he converts to pasture, and
starts a dairy or a beef cattle herd. Another section of his
land he plants in soybeans, or peanuts, or uses to produce

hay for outside sale. He has spread his market and weather risks. He now can afford to gamble on unusual success with his specialized crops.

Diversification in investments is also well known, especially in the form of the "investment trust."

For a long time, however, the tradition of American industry—heavy industry particularly—did not favor diversity. There have been exceptions, but this has been the rule. Steelmen stuck to steel, coal producers concentrated on coal exclusively; brewers and distillers, glassmakers and foundrymen did not as a rule go off into new fields. Indeed there is a general assumption among economists, publicists and trust busters that they couldn't if they wanted to, that "freedom of entry" by a newcomer into the large and long-established industries is *no longer possible.* Such is the recently stated conclusion of even so knowledgeable an economist as Professor Galbraith, in his refreshing book *American Capitalism* (Houghton Mifflin Co., 1952.) ". . . in an established industry," he writes, "where the scale of production is considerable, there is no such thing as freedom of entry. On the contrary, time and circumstances combine to bar the effective entry of new firms."

Nothing could be farther from the reality. Within the past decade, through diversification, new faces have characterized many segments of established American industry. The implications of this diversification upon the New Competition and on the function and utility of Bigness have hardly been noted. In my opinion they are very great.

The Celanese Corporation of America is one interesting example, of which there are many. This large enterprise for years had as its prime business the production of yarn used to make textile fibers. For raw materials for these yarns Celanese depended on cellulose, essentially purified wood pulp or cotton linters—the fuzzy "waste" that clings to the cottonseed. This cellulose material is treated with chemicals, so that it can then be spun into filaments or yarns.

Recently Celanese has entered the chemical business in a big way. Celanese is today a large producer of the so-called petro-chemicals (that is, chemicals made from petroleum or liquefied natural gas) and is engaged in extensive and costly research in this field. Some of the chemicals made by this "textile firm" are needed for making its basic product of fibers based on cellulose. But the production goes way beyond this, to include the *chemicals* needed for synthetic textiles.

The competition of these fibers based on chemicals with Celanese's cellulose-based materials doubtless accounts in part for this entry into a new industry. But in its chemical operations Celanese has now become a large producer of materials remote from fibers—glycols, formaldehyde, methanol, industrial alcohols, solvents and so on.

The fact is that a very large fiber concern has gone into quite another business, the general production and sale of industrial chemicals. This change in Celanese has strengthened competition quite outside and beyond the field of textile fibers.

Companies in entirely different fields—many of them relatively small—those engaged in the making of varnish, for example, and synthetic rubber or insecticides or plastics, now have in Celanese an additional and important potential source of their essential chemical materials.

Moreover, by Celanese's entry into the chemical business, it is just that much more difficult for any large chemical concern that was inclined to try it, to control industrial chemicals so as to lessen competition by small fabricators with its own finished products.

The entry of Celanese means that the established chemical-producing companies are under greater pressure to improve their own product, because still another large concern is now engaged in research and development and production of these materials. Diversification by Celanese, for its own corporate reasons of profit and stability and spreading of risks, has improved the competitive situation for a great many concerns as far away from textile fibers as one can imagine.

Distilling and the making of penicillin seem quite unrelated, industrially and in every other way. Yet Schenley Industries has put the two together. Schenley's subsidiary, Schenley Laboratories, Inc., is engaged in research, development and production of such antibiotic drugs as penicillin and streptomycin. The two fields are actually not so far apart as would at first appear. Schenley Industries has a backlog of experience and knowledge of the beneficial bacteria and molds. This is the foundation both of the ancient brewers' art and the ultramodern science of which penicillin and other "magic drugs" are examples.

Here again the effect of this diversification is to spur competition in the newer branches of the pharmaceutical industry. Whatever danger there may be of inertia or of monopoly control by the old-time drug concerns is lessened, the general public gets wider choice and other benefits of competition of ideas and of products.

The conservative coal-producing industry is one of the latest to join the movement toward diversification and thereby to become a big newcomer in an established industry. The Hanna interests of Ohio and Pennsylvania are an outstanding illustration. Here is a case of a historic coalminer moving into a wholly different field as a result of technical development and the pressure of the New Competition. This is taking place through the medium of the Pittsburgh Consolidation Coal Company, a Hanna concern.

If their first-rate research efforts prove economically successful, this coal company will shortly produce tar acids, then later chemicals based on these acids. It may ultimately become a producer of synthetic gasoline (made from coal) and synthetic gas, a large-scale producer of many of the so-called hydrocarbons which are among the building blocks of the plastics and synthetic fiber industries, now derived from some form of petroleum.

For the traditionally single-minded coal-producing industry to diversify in this way is a demonstration of the rapid change in our industrial pattern. Antitrust suits against big producers of chemical raw materials seem a feeble weapon indeed compared to the affirmative and competition-stimulating effects of this trend of diversification.

Entry into "pre-empted" fields of industry by newcomers to that field is commonly a consequence of research to find some use for the "waste products" of the industry, or some by-product that is surplus to the main line of the business. And it often happens that in order to make some important raw material—phenol, as an example—you must, in the operation, necessarily produce some materials not needed in your own business. So you decide to add that material to your line ("diversify"); this in turn may lead profitably into processing or fabrication of the "sideline" until it becomes a major interest. So a new entry into an established field is frequently not planned, in a business sense, but is more often a business follow-up of an idea or opportunity that first cropped up in the laboratory or development department. It s certainly true, however, that the fact that most successful businesses these days have substantial cash surpluses seeking profitable reinvestment in the business tremendously speeds up the diversification process.

The great paint and coating manufacturers, such as Glidden, National Lead Company, Sherwin-Williams, Eagle Picher, Du Pont, Pittsburgh Plate Glass Company, et al., provide other stimulating illustrations. Their product, paint, requires the use of vegetable oils from linseed, castor beans, cottonseed, soya, etc. Research on the leftovers, the "wastes," has led them into areas a long way from paint: vitamins, synthetic hormones, improved cattle feeds, molding compounds for plastic containers, etc. And since synthetic rubber materials are now found to be useful in paints, this has led the paint people into the field of chemicals from which rubber is made. The newer paint pigments tend to replace the traditional lead or zinc oxide with some of the new faces in the mineral world, such as titanium. So we find paint people, such as Glidden and Du Pont, entering the newest fields of metals, as miners or processors of titanium metals.

It is interesting to recall, as a historical footnote to "freedom of entry," that one of our largest and most enterprising textile producers of today entered that old-established field as a complete newcomer, through the route of dye production. I refer to Du Pont's nylon, which evolved out of basic research related to dyes, not textiles.

Other similar illustrations of new entries into established fields could be added from a score of different fields. Corn Products Company, Penick and Ford, Spencer Kellogg, A. E. Staley and other makers of sirup and such, use the cornstalks and corncobs—"waste" products—as the basis for moving into cellulose production, and from there to making plastics and other end products. Borden's and National Dairy, big milk producers, turn some of their "surplus" dairy output into the making of all manner of products such as adhesives, fibers, glues, etc. Amalgamated Sugar, a successful beet sugar concern produces amino acids out of "wastes," and from this produces food flavorings.

Food Machinery and Chemical Co., whose historic activity is making machinery for tinning or packing of vegetables and fruits, acquires a chemical company and becomes one of the country's largest producers of elemental phosphorus; this phosphorus it then uses to produce washing powders—so-called detergents, competing with the large soap concerns. Liquid Carbonic, Air Reduction and Union Carbide, having surplus carbonic acid from their main line of making great volumes of industrial gases, go into the "dry ice" business—this familiar product being solidified carbon dioxide.

And so the tale of diversification goes. One can keep up with it only by reading the daily news reports, so rapidly is this happening.

Taken together with the movement to integration, to which I shall refer in the following chapter (and with which it is closely related in its functioning), I am inclined to think that diversification—by increasing the freedom and extent of new entry into established business fields—is changing the dynamics of American industry and of the competitive system as much as any single development since the advent of mass production and mass marketing a generation ago.

The consequences will reach throughout industry and throughout business practices. This will be quite evident to the man on the street in the course of another five years or so. Hardly any phase of our economic life will be unaffected, but perhaps the chief consequence is as a part of the New Competition.

Bigness, and big research, are an integral part of this movement toward diversification. It is self-evident that only units with substantial resources, or small or medium units put together into larger ones, are able to accomplish major diversification of the kind I have described.

To try to dismiss this phenomenon as a process of "financial juggling" or "stock jobbing," or to try to spin out of it "suppression of competition" because mergers and acquisitions are often involved, is to miss the point of one of the significant developments in American economic life of this century.

8

Competition and Integration

THE New Competition has taken still another turn since trust busting was in its heyday. I refer to what is usually called "integration," though industrial independence might be a more descriptive term. Integration—in its current forms—constitutes, on the whole, a broadening, deepening and stepping-up of competition, and a consequent increased protection of the public.

Integration can be more understandably described than defined. Take by way of such an illustration the case of a long-established company whose name is a household synonym for matches—the Diamond Match Company. It required wood for the match sticks, phosphorus and other chemicals for the heads. At first it bought its supply of lumber and chemicals, largely confining itself to fabrication of the components into a match. Then it decided to own its own forests, produce its own lumber, and acquire timber reserves; it also built its own chemical plant to produce the material for the heads. In the language of the technical terminology, this change in scope of its business is "integration"; the more precise jargon for this particular expansion is "integration backward," that is, from the main product back to the necessary raw materials.

Later Diamond Match decided that to market its product adequately it needed some distribution outlets of its own, so that to production it added the function of distribution. This is also integration, and more technically "forward integration." Now, being in the lumber business, as an adjunct to producing billions of matchsticks, Diamond went into the lumber and building-materials business, setting up retail lumber yards; it also fabricates wood products, from window frames to tongue depressors.

Being in the timber business is not too long a step to producing wood pulp, and then products of wood pulp, from which paper matches are made; and being in the paper business Diamond goes on to make picnic paper plates, and so on. This can be described either as the "integration forward" of a big lumber and timber company, or "diversification" by a match company. This technical gobbledygook is not as academic and unimportant as it would seem—or perhaps as it should be. For a good share of the time and energy of the enforcement officers of this country's antitrust laws, of the Federal courts, and of the economists, lawyers and top executives of American industry have been devoted in the past three decades to many prolonged and exhausting attacks and defenses of "integration" in its many forms: backward, forward, vertical, horizontal and so on.

The subject of integration has infinite ramifications about which economic experts have written at great length. Opinions as to its desirability, from the public viewpoint, vary greatly. Although numerous particular instances to the contrary can be cited, it seems to me that, on balance, the over-all effect of industrial integration has been a strengthening of the New Competition.

Here again, Bigness plays an essential role, as is illustrated by the Ford Motor Company.

The Ford company must be able to have a continuous supply of the basic materials required for the building of an automobile or truck. If Ford's rivals can maintain for themselves an uninterrupted flow of all the many kinds of materials and components for automobiles, while Ford cannot, this would constitute, from the consumer's viewpoint, a *failure of the competitive system.* Per contra, anything that prevents such an interruption, or protects against it, tends to strengthen and fortify rivalry among auto manufacturers, and widens the area of choice of the prospective purchaser of cars.

(I am not here referring to limitations on supply of materials by direction of government, during a time of shortage due to war or defense preparations, but only to limitations resulting from competitive commercial forces.)

Generally speaking, there are two ways any large manufacturer can protect his vital lines of supply. One is by contract with suppliers of these individual items. The other is to supply itself from its *own* mines, steel plants, tire factories and so on. The latter course, if carried very far, creates vexing problems. Many executives believe that it creates more troubles than it solves, generally speaking; but it does provide a great measure of freedom and independence in the competitive struggle.

At the height of its growth the Ford Motor Company

for many years carried integration a long way, purchasing coal fields, extensive timber holdings, railroads, river tows and barges. It is hard to conceive of any action looking toward self-sufficiency in the fierce competition among auto makers that Ford's policy did not anticipate. Although since World War II the company has come to rely more heavily than before on contractual agreements with multiple suppliers, Ford recently announced plans for construction of plants in northern Michigan to recover iron from low-grade ores, for use in its own steel production.

Not many industrial concerns have carried industrial independence, during its period of greatest expansion, as far as Ford did, and, of course, few have the resources or the inclination to do so. But the illustrations, throughout industry, of some degree or other of industrial self-sufficiency are numerous indeed; the integration principle has been adopted to a marked extent throughout almost every sector of American business. Durez Plastics, which once bought all its raw materials, now makes its own phenol, formaldehyde, etc. Most brewers now themselves make the yeast and corn products they need. Several very large electric utilities develop their own coal supplies. Fertilizer concerns more and more do their own mining and processing of the raw phosphate or potash ore, rather than buy it from others.

The business reasons behind integration are many and varied; for example, such self-sufficiency may give a better cost than outside purchase; it may add a profit on an intermediate step in production; it may give greater stability of labor policy and hence of production. Whatever the reasons, the effect on competition has been direct and significant.

Integration has heightened the vitality and increased the fluidity of business competition, because, like diversification it has led to the entry into established industry of newcomers. Thus (as with diversification) new strong factors have been introduced into what might otherwise conceivably become a static or complacent industry, and thereby the public interest has been protected and competition promoted.

At times the effect of integration in stimulating competition is overlooked because of preoccupation with the *form* it takes, rather than the substance. In 1952, as an example, General Motors, among the country's largest consumers of steel, consummated a contract with the Jones & Laughlin Steel Company. The steel company—one of the big six—agreed to construct a new plant, the entire output to be exclusively for General Motors' account. But the $28,000,000 for the new plant was financed entirely by G.M., not by Jones & Laughlin. Fully as much as if G.M. had itself built a steel plant (as Ford has) G.M., by this arrangement, is integrating its automobile production by securing an independent supply of steel. Both Ford, with its own steel plants, and G.M. under this arrangement, have made entry into the steel business, in the practical sense of adding to the competitive pressures on the long-established steel companies.

Some economists hold that there is a difference in the effect on competition between these two cases: (1) that of a concern that has been buying its steel but then shifts over to producing a supply for its own use exclusively, and (2) a new steel concern entering the field. But by the workaday test of actual effect on competition, and on the protection of the public from trends toward lethargy, inefficiency or monopoly, the difference is not consequential, it seems to me. Any businessman who has been accustomed to selling his product to X, Y and Z will be hard to persuade that the competitive situation has not been stepped up if one day X announces that he is no longer in the buying market, but is setting up a plant to serve all or part of his own needs.

As a part of the New Competition, there are several other forms of integration, or industrial independence, the net effect of which is to make competition more lively. Thus, to secure market acceptance of a new kind of product—the first electric refrigerator, or the first kitchen waste-food disposal appliance, or a new drug, for examples —it is not enough for a manufacturer to make a good product. A great deal of advertising and sales and educational effort and expenditure that the distributor or the retailer may not be willing to assume is required, or the new product dies on the vine.

Or it may be that the new product—the television receiver or oil-burner furnace in their inception, for example —is one that should have the kind of servicing that does not exist among distributors. Or it may be that the manufacturer's competitors may have pretty well sewed up the distributor and retailer field.

In such cases, it may not be enough, in the interest of competition, for the manufacturer to be independent in his sources of supply; he may also have to "integrate forward" and have a hand in the distribution function, even at times dealing directly with the customer, if the customer is to get the full benefit of the new product.

As I have said, this integration, or move toward self-sufficiency, often resembles a phase of diversification. The making of airplanes illustrates the point. A large airplane requires scores of electronic devices with intricate wiring circuits. Most of these devices are developed and supplied by the country's large and enterprising electronics manufacturers, General Electric, Westinghouse, Radio Corporation of America and so on.

But most large airplane manufacturers also have extensive electronics departments of their own, fully manned and equipped for the specialized electronics needs of their aircraft. In a sense this is diversification—airplane makers in the electronics business. But it is also a manifestation of the extensive movement toward industrial independence. If the time ever comes when competitors tried to cut into their supply of these vital devices, or otherwise restricted their availability, this independence in electronics would stand the airplane makers in good stead. Or if the electronics companies did not move ahead in research and development to suit the needs of aeronautics, the airplane makers would not be without a way of spurring them on.

This same principle obtains in many other fields of industry. Getting exclusive control of any vital industrial material or component today is thereby most difficult, not so much because of the Sherman Act, but because of conditions built into present-day industry.

9

Competition and the One Big Market

THE territorial United States is the biggest unified free market the world has ever seen: biggest in geographic extent, in total dollar volume, in variety, in the proportion of individuals with good incomes—a very important point. It is by all odds the most highly competitive market, in the sense that the customers are subjected to stimuli from all sides that make them very conscious of the relative and comparative merits of various products, or to alternative ways of spending their income.

The United States then is one big market, the first of its kind in history.

For a manufacturing business to stay alive in a localized market, or even a regional one, it has only to keep up with local or regional competitors. This, roughly, was the status of competition in the days when we were still predominantly an agricultural country, when the Sherman Act was debated and passed, and indeed until the advent of the New Competition about thirty years ago.

In manufacturing, it is rapidly coming to be true that to stay alive and prosper a manufacturing concern must be prepared to meet competition coming to its prospective customers from any place within the one big market which is the U.S.A.

No part of the big market can be ignored, and new technical developments frequently have this very thing in mind—to enable a producer economically to reach further and further into the national market.

Take such a traditionally localized product as milk. When I lived in Valparaiso, Indiana, as a boy, milk deliveries were not even town-wide, but a matter of the capacity of your neighbor's cow. Milk now has become regionalized, by rapid transport; a new development to can fresh milk may put it on a national market.

And if the customers (individuals or corporate) cannot be reached and fought for because of transport costs, or other reasons, a branch plant or assembly point is set up in the locality or region. For example, the smaller communities of the country are dotted with local Coca-Cola and other beverage bottling works, parts of national businesses.

As a consequence of competition for the one big market, localized manufacturing with a localized market is more and more becoming an exception, and its economic difficulties within its own market, as against national competition, grow all the time. Small localized manufacture's function is coming to be that of a *supplier* to some national business, a Big Business, or the producer of specialized items—such as dies—for large enterprise. Such large firms as Standard Oil of New Jersey, General Electric, General Motors, R.C.A. and hundreds of others provide a market for thousands of small, even very small, manufacturers of single components of the larger company's products. This in part accounts for the remarkable vitality of small-plant manufacture of specialized items.

To compete in the big market takes Bigness. What makes for size, then, is the big market. We need Big Business for a big country.

Bigness is a consequence of modern machinery, modern industrial research and big struggles for nationwide markets. Where a country's economy is characterized by the small local manufacturer and the small local market which he serves with only local competition, if any, we have, typically, what we call "backward" or "underdeveloped" areas."

The effects of littleness in business upon social and political fragmentation, and the contrasting *unifying consequences of Bigness*, present an aspect of my theme that deserves far more attention from scholars and men of affairs than it has received thus far. To those liberals who distrust the idea of Bigness in business, but who see in the Schuman-Monnet Coal-Steel Plan the beginning of real hope for a politically unified Europe, I commend the implications of these recent words of the president of Centre Technique des Industries de la Fonderie, the French industrialist M. Pierre Ricard:

> . . . a single steel enterprise in America produces by itself and solely within the United States as much steel as is produced in the whole area covered by the Schuman Plan, where production is broken down into a hundred independent companies, scattered over six countries, each of which has political, social, fiscal and monetary autonomy.*

* Quoted in the *London Economist* for December 15, 1951, page 1464.

10

Internal Competition

A FORM of the New Competition that has in recent years taken on major importance may be called internal. It is competition, on a formal and self-conscious basis, *between* units within a large organization, one against the others, as distinguished from competition between that organization and its economic rivals.

To a certain degree, of course, this is an old story. But with the growth of very large enterprises, with a great variety of entirely different and often functionally competitive products or services, there has arisen to a point of major internal corporate policy this within-the-family kind of competition, between units of the organization, between products that are in a different or the same price or quality range. General Motors' Chevrolet dealers, for example, have had tough competition from G.M.'s Pontiac. The same company's Buick competes with its Oldsmobile, above it in price, and its Pontiac below.

In some very large concerns internal competition is such that if a raw materials department cannot meet an outsider's price or quality for chemicals, say, needed by another department, that department, as a matter of company policy, will go out and buy the chemicals where the price and quality are better, even if it buys from a concern that is its warmest competitor.

It is common, of course, to find rivalry *between operating units* within one corporate family, as a means of maintaining the highest performance. Thus the separate operating units of the Bell System are in efficiency competition with each other, even though each, within its geographic area, is a legal monopoly without any competition. The operating costs, overheads, and all the various indicia of performance of the Wisconsin Telephone Company, as an example, is a competitive measure of performance of the Illinois Bell, or any other separate unit of the system. Knox hats and Dobbs hats are both owned by the same concern, the Hat Corporation of America. In one hat store you are told Knox is the best in the world; a hat store across the street says it is Dobbs, and the competition between the two to cover your head is so vigorous most people would not believe they are part of the same company.

Such intramural competition extends beyond products and performance figures, to ideas and ways of thinking. It provides a means of policy criticism, and the testing of efficiency, of great value; thus the competition of ideas between the research scientists and the development engineers, between production men and sales forces, etc.

This kind of organized family competition is almost inevitable with size, as the organization charts of any of our larger companies will make clear at a glance. Many of these biggest of the big are not monolithic economic units, but have come to resemble a kind of federal system in business. The major divisions of product or service, each with its separate general manager and staff officers, have many characteristics of separate companies; at the same time they have a unity, bound together closely on those matters which are of common concern or common policy, not wholly unlike the structural relation of our states to the national government.

This matter of internal competition is a development of management of big enterprises that deserves more study and attention than it has received, not only as a move toward managerial decentralization, but as a significant form of modern competition.

11

Advertising and Competition

THE highly competitive atmosphere and tempo of American business, and of American life in general, is one of its most obvious characteristics. Selling activity, and particularly the form known as advertising, has ceased to be a mere adjunct of commerce (as it was in the days of the early trust busters); it has become a major industry in its own right.

Advertising on this tremendous scale has become a new and important factor in widening the range and freedom of choice we Americans enjoy.

A considerable portion of advertising is probably wasteful because ineffective, and some even is in bad taste. But it is clear to me that advertising, as an instrument of modern industry, stimulates and creates innovation. As such it is a major force in maintaining and strengthening the New Competition.

It has made us sensitive to the merits, or claimed merits, of products that compete for our dollars. It has made domination of a market by some "conspiracy" of insiders extremely difficult, if not impossible. It has kept the average man alert and demanding, so that he expects and gets a stream of new products and a diversity of goods and services unknown in earlier days, and quite without precedent anywhere else in the world.

For the purpose of analyzing the effect of Bigness on competition I found it convenient to accept the assumption that competition is always desirable in and of itself, that, therefore, anything which in any degree dilutes or impairs its full force and effect is bad. This is an extreme view, however, and one I do not share.

Competition—getting ahead of the other fellow—is by no manner of means the *only* powerful incentive in the American industrial system. Moreover, our belief in competition is not an absolute one: in large sectors of our system we have severely modified competition—the so-called "fair trade" laws—or even eliminated direct competition, as in the field of public utilities and carriers.

Competition is not regarded by us as an end, but only a means to an end. The end is to achieve a certain kind of society and a kind of individual life which to us seems desirable.

PART III

THE FRUITS OF BIGNESS

Introduction

TO THOSE individuals who are deeply distrustful of business in its effects on human welfare and values, the question whether Big Business has in fact brought benefits—both material and intangible—to the people of the country "has nothing to do with the case."

Such skepticism and even cynicism toward business and businessmen has articulate present-day spokesmen. They are the legatees of centuries of aversion, disbelief and rejection of the ethical and cultural standards of businessmen, expressed not only by political leaders but also by great imaginative writers—novelists, playwrights, satirists, poets and religious seers.

As a consequence a deeply held dogma exists; to those who are its current adherents, evidence of the actual benefits conferred by Big Business is neither persuasive nor even relevant. They will be no more persuaded by a recital of such testimony than will dogmatic extremists about government be willing to weigh, open-mindedly, whether or not creative consequences flow from some of the newer functions of government.

Our basic economic laws, as they are now construed and applied to Big Business, reflect very largely this dogmatic indifference to results and performance. The fact that a Big

Business *in fact* is benefiting the country is waved aside as irrelevant in determining whether that business should be divided up or restrained. To them the important thing is the iron law, not the living breathing facts of life. The "rule of reason" of the earlier days of our fight on monopoly has become attenuated by the rule of dogma.

This rigidity, however, is not typical of the way the great body of laymen think. For by and large we are a country of reasonable and moderate people, always open to reason *on the basis of results*. We say "you've got to show me"—but we are ready to be shown.

In this book I direct myself to those who by habit look at the results, the actual consequences of Bigness as they appear in our daily lives.

12

Bigness for National Security

WITH the single exception of the effect of Bigness upon the individual, national security is the most important test of the principle and practice of Bigness in contemporary American life.

To the extent that the principle of Bigness, in our economic life, contributes in an affirmative and an indispensable way to the strengthening of our national security we should, by an explicit and affirmative national policy, encourage and protect that kind of Bigness.

In this decade of danger, productivity in turning out a prodigious flow of armament and developing new scientific weapons is the most important single test of the utility of Bigness in serving the national security. But it is not the sole test. Offsetting factors must be counted, too, in reaching a general judgment, or in particular cases. For example, is productivity by Bigness achieved at the expense of a physically dangerous overconcentration of industry in already highly concentrated areas? Is it at the expense of labor-management tensions of a hazardous kind? Does Big Business demand armament profits so exorbitant as to destroy confidence and support for the defense effort among many people? These are relevant factors in judging the effectiveness of Big Business.

Whether Bigness is an impediment to national security, or whether it is in most vital regions literally indispensable to it, should be measured by thinking of "national security" in the broadest sense. It is not only a matter of the manufacture of tanks and armor plate and bazookas and all the tens of thousands of items required for our military forces and those of our friends who depend upon us for arms. Our security also requires high productivity of the "civilian" goods and services essential for the health and vigor of our country. Moreover, we are now agreed, in principle at least, that economic aid to free peoples in Europe and Asia is in a very immediate sense part of the strengthening of our own security.

It is in these broader terms that I think we should weigh the issue of Bigness and national security.

My own opportunities for close observation in this area cover the fifteen-year period of 1937-1952. During all but the last two years of this fifteen-year period I was in the public service, with responsibility for some aspects of national security.

My work both in TVA and the Atomic Energy Commission involved the production of strictly military defense materials (in TVA, ammonium nitrate and elemental phosphorus, both munitions; in AEC, atomic bombs). It also involved the widest ramifications of a defense program, such as planning for and producing electric power for aluminum, finding ways of stimulating food production, and so on. Dealings with hundreds of different kinds of business organizations, involving in total several billions of dollars, on specific and concrete matters of production, were the grist of the work of myself and my associates.

From my own experience I conclude that Big Business and the principles and techniques of Bigness are indispensable to our security. Accordingly, I believe that our national laws, our national climate of opinion, and the attitude of our public servants should be consistent with that conclusion.

This is not always the case. I can illustrate by a single experience, out of many, from my work as chairman of the Atomic Energy Commission. The case involves a vital security interest, namely the last step in the production of atomic bombs, which is the fabrication of the components, and their assembly into a workable weapon.

On January 1, 1947, the new civilian Atomic Energy

Commission took over the responsibilities of atomic weapon development and production from the Army's Manhattan District. By this time many of the great scientists who had actually fabricated the first bombs had returned to their various laboratories. But a superb scientific team remained in Los Alamos, on a mountaintop in New Mexico, carrying on the fundamental work. We new commissioners took our first look into the secret bomb-storage areas.

The result was a shock. The substantial stockpile of atom bombs we and the top military assumed was there, in readiness, did not exist. Furthermore, the production facilities that might enable us to produce quantities of atomic bombs so engineered that they would not continue to require a Ph.D. in physics to handle them in the field, likewise did not exist. No quantity production of these weapons was possible under the existing "handicraft" setup.

To redesign the bomb so it would be a genuine field weapon, to carry forward fundamental work on new designs, to design and build a plant in which this infinitely complex thing could be put into quantity industrial-type production, and then to operate such a factory required talents in an unusual and remarkable combination.

First of all, this task required *industrial* experience. What we wanted was not something that could be done in a laboratory alone, but in a production center, with factory techniques, factory mechanics (of a high order of skill, it is true) and factory management.

Second, what we wanted done required men of a high order of ability in scientific fundamentals, equal to any in the universities but also experienced in dealing with industrial problems and with industrial associates.

Third, this task called for a special kind of operating experience in dealing with the technical characteristics of systems used in these weapons, and others then actively under development, new weapons which have since been proof-tested.

Most important of all, these three capabilities of research, industrial techniques and operation had to be *combined* in the same team, with experience in working together as a unit.

To go out and create such an organization was out of the question. There was not time.

It was our "hunch" that there was such an organization in existence—the Bell System, that is, the team consisting of the American Telephone & Telegraph Company and its associated operating companies, together with the Bell Laboratories, a research and development institution, and Western Electric, the manufacturing arm of the system.

A careful analysis confirmed this initial "hunch." I spent Decoration Day of 1949 with the president of A. T. & T., the late Leroy Wilson. On behalf of President Truman and the Atomic Energy Commission, I requested that A. T. & T., Bell Laboratories and Western Electric, as a team, take the heavy responsibility which I have here summarized. Mr. Wilson said that his company was already committed to important defense work, and while it did not relish another great load such as this, the Bell System would accept the assignment as in the national interest.

Then he said (and I paraphrase only): the government

is asking the Bell System to put its research-manufacturing-
operation setup to work on this task because it is a combination of these things that you regard as essential to the
nation's security. I must tell you, he said, that a few months
ago the government, through the Antitrust Division of the
Department of Justice, filed a suit under the Sherman Antitrust Act to sever the Western Electric from the Bell
System, as well as to split up Western Electric into several
parts. What the government asks in this lawsuit, Mr. Wilson
indicated, is that the courts break up and dissolve the very
organizational unity and size you say this vital security job
requires. The fairness of telephone rates, including the
cost of Western Electric equipment, Mr. Wilson said, is
regulated by the states and the Federal Communications
Commission. What the Antitrust Division charges is essentially that this team we have put together is too big, and
should be made smaller.

The Bell System took over the Sandia operation (as this
part of atomic weapons production is called) not long after
my meeting with Mr. Wilson. It has been responsible
for it ever since. The stepped-up production of atomic
bombs and the favorable results in the tests of new weapons,
as officially announced from time to time, are, I am sure,
in considerable measure due to the unique contribution of
the Bell System and of the great scientific talents in the
Los Alamos laboratory.

The antitrust suit to break up the Bell System is pend-
ing, and is being prepared for trial.

There may be those who would say: But in the end the
Bell System may win its case in the courts; and in any case,

win or not, it certainly will be five years or more before a final decision to sever the Bell System is rendered in the Supreme Court. How then is the atomic bomb program injured *now*, how is our nation's security impaired *now*, by a possible dismemberment that may not transpire for years, if ever?

The answer may not be obvious to anyone not aware of the prodigious human demands on a company's management that preparation for such a great litigation entails, or of the morale consequences on management of the possibility hanging over them of an enforced reorganization of the whole enterprise.

A terrible pressure of work falls upon the most responsible men both in management and in technical pursuits in such large organizations as A. T. & T. and the many others, public and private, that carry much of the heavy job of keeping this country's technical weapons at the highest possible level. The figures of American production of civilian goods *plus* prodigious technical feats of armament need to be translated into terms of the toll they exact on men.

The preparation of the company's side of a suit such as the Bell case, involving as it does the technical side of the business and going back into transactions and decisions of many years ago, requires countless hours of work by the top-level executives and technicians who participated in those decisions. Since men of these attainments and experience are few in number, since they cannot wholly delegate this task of preparation to others (it is they who know most of the surrounding circumstances), both the preparation for a crucial lawsuit and the urgent work of the government's defense program suffer, inevitably, for even the strongest men have limits to their stamina.

This example of the Bell System—and there are other recent instances, with grave implications for national security—presents one of the strongest possible reasons for an early and rigorous re-examination of our whole public policy and public attitudes toward Bigness.

13

Bigness for Individual Security

JUST as we insist that our country be secure, in a military sense, against the hazards that lie in wait for us as a nation, we have also, in more recent years, adopted another kind of security as a goal: individual economic security. How has Bigness as a characteristic of business furthered this objective?

Take year-round employment for industrial workers, as an example. Our desire for a stable and humane social system leads us to seek to reach this most difficult of objectives.

Here and there quite small businesses, by superior management, have made excellent headway in this direction.

As a broad proposition, however (in industries of seasonal demand in particular), Bigness is necessary to accomplish the necessary planning of production, and the requisite influence upon purchaser habits and distribution practices. To smooth out the dips of employment it is often necessary to be able to stockpile or accumulate large inventories or to shift from one kind of product to another for a temporary period, or to move into markets in widely separated parts of the country or even of the world. Only a business of substantial size can do this.

A stable and humane society is one that recognizes the individual's natural desire for a measure of security and peace of mind in old age. Such a society will favor an industrial system that can provide extensive and liberal pensions. Such pension systems, ideally, should, I think, be designed as much as possible to be a cost of the particular business, rather than chiefly a cost assessed against everyone through taxes. In this way it becomes a challenge to management's skill, and a part of the system of incentives and rewards by which management and organized labor can improve the general health of the particular business or industry.

Some small business units have provided excellent pension systems. But here again, as a broad proposition, the outstanding pensions plans are those of larger enterprises. That these plans often did not originate with enlightened management, that their adoption often required the force of legislation (opposed by many big concerns) and the pressure of union activity, is certainly true; but the results are now the important thing. The resulting pension plans are good, and no one but extremists will ever try to do away with them.

As a youth I lived and worked for a time in Gary, Indiana. In the great U.S. Steel mills at that time the working hours were 13½ hours a day one week, and 11½ hours the alternate week, *seven days a week*. Now, due largely to unionization, governmental action and managerial enlightenment, steelworkers at Gary receive retirement pensions—to say nothing of short hours, high wages and vacations with pay. Big Business of even a generation ago and today operate in two entirely different worlds.

One of the most remarkable and most heartening chapters of social history is the evolution of the relations between employers and employees in American industry to their present stage of development.

In this country at mid-century the idea of "class war" as a means of improving the lot of workers—an idea that once had a thriving start—has almost entirely disappeared. Efforts by management to suppress and destroy independent labor unions by almost any means, including violence, espionage, corruption of union officers and economic coercion, have become rare.

With all its painful and obvious limitations, this record is one of the greatest achievements of American democracy. Moreover, to the extent that the individual worker is increasingly protected from the exercise of *arbitrary* power of his supervisor or employer—the very essence of freedom in the earning of one's living—and has an effective voice in the running of his union's affairs, this accomplishment to date, crude and unfinished as it is, takes its place with some of the greatest in the history of individual freedom.

But this development is only at its beginning. There will be setbacks now and then; but the most constructive and creative period is still before us.

Taking the picture as a whole, the most potent leadership—in unions and in management—in this marked social change has been found in companies of substantial size. (The outstanding exception is probably the women's and men's clothing industry, where small units are common.) A generation ago about the worst instances of suppression and coercion by management and class-warfare tactics and violence by unions occurred in our largest industries— steel and automobiles, for example. Today, the reverse is true.

On May 23, 1950, an agreement was entered into between one of America's biggest of Big Businesses, General Motors, and the United Auto Workers (CIO). In a number of respects this contract represents a pioneer undertaking. Its term, for example, is without precedent: for five years both the business and the union agree to abide by the agreement "without reopening by either party for any cause." This agreement embodied an explicit recognition by General Motors of the dollars-and-cents value of responsibility by a labor union. Charles Wilson, head of G.M., was not niggardly in giving credit to the union; the company could never have made the agreement, he said, had the union not "demonstrated . . . its sincerity and responsibility in carrying out agreements in the past."

The agreement included provisions against hazards to life and health, and for pensions, hospital coverage and vacations. In addition to an adjustment of wages each three months in accordance with changes in the cost of living, the contract included a much-praised and also much-criticized "improvement factor." Four cents per hour was to be added to all wages, annually, throughout the period of the contract. But the *reasoning* behind this provision gives it its long-range importance. The contracting parties, management and labor, used the following words in the agreement itself:

The annual improvement factor provided herein recognizes that a continuing improvement in the standard of living of employees depends upon technological progress, better tools, methods, processes and equipment and a co-operative attitude on the part of all parties in such progress. It further recognizes the principle that to produce more with the same amount of human effort is a sound economic and social objective.

Commenting on this provision the president of G.M. said: "Both parties completely accept the principle of progress, including the use of machines, mechanical power and better organization, better working conditions and better arrangement of the work in order not to waste human effort."

14

Productivity and Bigness

MY RESPONSIBILITY, as a public servant, for industrial operations, and my study of areas outside my own direct experience have convinced me that the encouragement of Bigness is essential if we are to maintain the highest levels of production and the lowest costs of *basic industrial commodities.*

Iron- and steelmaking are examples. In this country, until about a hundred years ago, iron- and steelmaking were carried on by many plants. Each of these numerous plants was small. As a consequence of technical developments and the great expansion in the market for all kinds of steel products, this situation changed completely. As we produced more and more tons of pig iron, the *number* of the iron- and steelmaking furnaces decreased, and the size of the individual furnaces grew. This trend continues until our day, when we have witnessed a spectacular increase in the total productiveness of the country and in the size of the individual furnaces.

As things stand today, and for the next decade or so at least, to get high productivity and low cost of iron and steel, we must have big machinery—even bigger than at present perhaps. This requires the resources and managerial scope of big companies, with earnings adequate to attract the vast capital expenditures required.

Much the same thing is true in another field of production, one upon which most of America's modern industry —and her security and living standards—is built. I refer to the production of electrical energy, public and private, whether created by water power, or by using coal, gas or oil as the fuel for operating a steam turbine. (This is, of course, not a competitive industry, but one of legal, regulated monopoly.)

We eat up electric power at an unbelievable rate; in my opinion this trend will continue for an almost indefinite period.

It is not easy to comprehend the change in our *rate* of

use of electricity. In 1936, TVA's Norris Dam was considered a large addition to the nation's power supply. The late Wendell Willkie vigorously contended, in 1933, that Norris Dam should not be built because it would create a big "surplus" of electricity. The water wheels and power generators, two in number, had a total capacity of 100,000 kilowatts.

Norris Dam is only one—and not one of the very largest —of more than a score of such structures built since that time by TVA. Today, to meet prodigious atomic energy plant requirements, TVA is also installing new coal-burning, power-generating facilities (the individual generators now grown from 50,000 to 200,000 kilowatts with the most recent order being for 250,000 kilowatts in a single machine) that in total represent more power capacity than *thirty* Norris Dams. Just to keep up with the normal increase in annual needs of power, for the same region for which Norris Dam was built, will require new power plants the equivalent of *seven* Norris Dams *each year*.

I cite these figures from this one relatively small region only as illustrative of what is going on by way of increasing demands for electricity in almost every other part of the country. By 1970, America's electrical energy output will probably be more than doubled over 1950.

It is at last becoming clear that electricity is so fundamental to the life of the nation that no one should ever concern himself about a "surplus." Electricity in great quantities, at low cost, creates its own market, creates new uses and new productivity, which in turn creates further need for more electricity.

These comments about electric supply go to the heart of the issue of Bigness. For it takes Bigness of individual power units, Bigness of power-supplying enterprises and Bigness of electric equipment companies to create the huge pools of power we need, timed for our needs, and at low cost.

To build turbines and generators of this mammoth size and their ever-bigger transmission equipment requires Bigness in the manufacturing company—Bigness of research, development and production. To operate units of this size and their transmission systems that are required to move the blocks of power calls for a big electric enterprise, whether it be a TVA or Bonneville Administration, a Pacific Gas & Electric or a Commonwealth Edison.

Similar considerations apply to basic minerals. The maintenance of the United States as a going concern requires almost unbelievably large quantities of iron ore, copper, bauxite (for aluminum), petroleum, coal, phosphate and other raw minerals. It is not simply that it would be "a nice thing" to have these. We *must* have them to live, and in quantities that not many years ago would have seemed out of the question. But looking ahead a single generation, to the year 1975, the prospect for basic life-essential minerals presents a challenging picture.

The problem has three principal parts.

First, we must explore for and discover and develop our remaining raw minerals lying within the United States, and do so in the most effective way possible. For their development the best engineering and business practice is required.

Second, where our American reserves of high-grade materials are nearing an end—iron and copper ores are outstanding examples—we must develop technical means of utilizing ores of constantly lower and lower concentration, at costs that are bearable. Well utilized, we have the technical and business talents to stretch our low-grade home supplies for a very long time. This will require huge outlays of private capital, and call for great adjustments within industry and in many communities.

Third, we need to increase the already vast activity directed toward exploring, developing and transporting to our shores raw materials mined in other parts of the world.

To meet this major and overshadowing problem of basic resources our government, of course, has vital roles to play; but for end results we must, in the main, rely upon Big Business. The magnitude of private resources required for this task, the managerial complexity of the problem and the high responsibilities assumed when operations go on in other countries—such as the development of oil in the Middle East and of oil and iron ore in Venezuela—make this problem essentially one for very large mature enterprises. They need to be well led, by responsible and modern-minded men—generally but not universally the case today. But in any case, they must be big.

15

Bigness and the Distribution of Goods and Credit

AS I have traveled about the parts of the world which are clinical cases of poverty, uncleanliness and the most undemocratic disparity between classes—the most utterly poor and the most conspicuously rich—what impressed me greatly was not a lack of natural resources or favorable climate, or an uneducable people: it was that these people have suffered most grievously from lack of a sensible and efficient system of *distribution* of goods.

America's progress, economically, can be told in considerable measure by our advance in the techniques of distribution, as the unhappy condition of the Middle East or Latin America is attributable in substantial measure to a debilitating and static system of distribution. The terrible toll of the poor man's substance that their miserable distribution systems exact is one of the saddest commentaries on the lives of at least half the people of the world today. If a fraction of the indignation expended on the unquestionably archaic land laws of these backward countries was directed toward improving the inefficient distribution system, faster progress would be made all along the line. And what is the most obvious functional characteristic of distribution in these regions? It is the *smallness* of individual units.

The story in America and in Britain and parts of Europe is different. Big Business must receive the major credit for leadership in these great achievements in distribution.

When buying a product at an American store, Mr. and Mrs. Consumer have to pay about as much for the cost of getting that commodity from the factory or farm as it cost to produce it in the first place. The product must usually weave its way through a maze of wholesalers, jobbers, distributors and retail stores until at last it slides across the store counter, or the delivery truck deposits it at the customer's door. Nothing is more important to the budget and living standards of the average family than ways and means, if possible, of cutting these costs of distribution.

To whittle down this high proportion of the "cost of living" involved in getting their product into people's hands is a major preoccupation of a large segment of American men of business.

It is here—in distribution—that Bigness has made what is perhaps its most spectacular change in the face of everyday American life. I refer, of course, to the chain store. It is only somewhat more than one generation ago that the distribution of goods was almost entirely in the hands of local "department stores" or small independent retail stores.

Once the independent merchant was the prime representative of middle-class life in most parts of the United

States. The waning of his importance has had important effects on economic thinking and on politics. How deeply —even bitterly—this strong and highly respected group of merchants resented the inroads of the chain store is difficult to understand in a time when the A&P, the Penney Stores, Sears Roebuck, Montgomery Ward and a multitude of other chain establishments are to be found in every city and town in America. That feeling still persists to some degree, but cannot compare in intensity to that which I remember as a youth in a Midwestern small town of forty years ago.

How could it happen that the chain-store system would grow and prosper despite the great political strength and warm popular sympathy enjoyed by the independent merchant and grocer?

It is difficult to escape the conclusion that, on the whole, Bigness won because it did a good job for the buying public.

Bigness, in getting goods to people, has proved to the customer that it can cut the cost of distribution for essential commodities. Big Business in distribution has helped mightily to make foods once seasonal or local or only for the rich widely available to almost all economic groups in all corners of the country. It has been a main factor in improving the human and hygienic conditions under which all goods, and particularly foods, are supplied to people. These are by no means "merely" economic gains: these represent practical workaday applications of democratic aspirations.

In my opinion, therefore, those antitrust prosecutions

and proceedings, and actions in Congress, which, in effect, are leveled against the mass production and mass distribution of goods by chain-store systems, in the end will fail. There is a simple reason for this: Bigness in distribution is in the consumer's interest, by and large.

It has also been in the interest of employees. Take the number of hours stores used to be open for business in the days before the chain stores, when the owner-operated small store was the rule. They were, characteristically, open from early morning until eight or nine o'clock at night, even later on Saturdays; the hours of labor of the proprietor and the "clerks" were outrageously long and wearying.

What of the part played by the chain-store method of distribution in improving the hygienic conditions in the distribution of foodstuffs? Today, in the chain-store period of grocery stores, very few foods are sold in bulk. An actual cracker barrel, symbol of social "argufying" in the small-town grocery store, is no longer to be seen; and similarly the sugar barrel, the tea and coffee bin, the bulk sale of butter and lard and a hundred other staples. We have Bigness largely to thank for this major improvement. A similar comment could be made about the great improvement in cleanliness in handling meat and milk today, compared to the days when these products were distributed almost exclusively by the small operator of a butcher shop or a "creamery."

My own observation has been that in many—though not in all—areas, the chain-store technique of organization has in fact reduced the cost of distribution of many products, and improved the human setting of the distribution of goods in our country. The personal relation between the storekeeper and the customer, and the active participation of local store managers in community affairs—where most chain establishments have in the past certainly fallen short—is apparently on its way toward improvement.

It is now quite well understood that mass distribution has contributed greatly to the competitive system and to our standard of living. But the beneficial effect of improved methods of distribution upon *production* of these goods is little comprehended. The most notable instance I know of is that of Sears Roebuck & Company. Although Sears itself has grown bigger and bigger, both as merchandiser and manufacturer, its policies have resulted in the creation of many new, small manufacturers, and greater stability for existing smaller concerns from which it buys; these suppliers now number about 20,000. Departing from an earlier preoccupation with price alone, Sears has come also to stress the quality of the products of its suppliers.

Almost of equal importance has been the effect of this huge business in improving the management skills of small manufacturers from whom they buy the thousands of items one finds in their catalogue and in their retail outlets throughout the world. This development of Sears' policy, both here and abroad, has done much for the modernizing of the management of smaller manufacturers, teaching them how to do a better job of production, cost keeping, etc., and making available to them the benefits of research and engineering.

What Bigness has done to improve the distribution of goods it shows promise of doing in the quite different but equally vital area of the improved "distribution" of credit.

Making credit and banking services more responsive to Mr. Average Citizen's needs, making them serve him more intelligently and at low cost, are gains Bigness can render that may prove as significant for the public and for business enterprise as those secured through the advent and influence of the chain-store system.

The small businessman, in particular, has need of a banking and credit system big enough to spread risks and thus keep down the cost of credit to him, equipped with enough specialized knowledge and services to help him with his own special credit problems, and localized into even the smallest community. Such credit facilities may mean for the small enterprise the difference between failing and prospering.

I have remarked that in poverty-stricken countries smallness is the mark of the corrosive and inefficient systems of distribution of goods; so it is also with their banking and credit systems. Usurious moneylenders, who prey on the needs of the helpless and who contribute little to the country's development, are the rule; banking and credit as a constructive, imaginative and enterprise-irrigating function rarely exists. It was a pernicious credit system that as much as any single cause held back the people of the South for almost fifty years after the Civil War, tying many of them to a decaying cotton economy, delaying the growth of a diversified agriculture and retarding industry and commerce. Such a suffocating credit system was not a plot hatched by a big banking combine; it was the product of small, provincial credit monopolies.

The American credit picture today is in marked contrast to this sterile and inhumane picture. It is characterized by remarkable and increasing diversity and freedom of choice for the man or business in need of credit. There are now several places to which an individual may freely turn for his credit needs, whether for personal loans—funds for a new house or for a new refrigerator—or for his small business or his farm. There are many alternatives open to businessmen or public bodies if the credit required is very large, for a mine or manufacturing plant or a super-highway system or city water-supply.

Never have there been more avenues of credit, private, mutual nonprofit, co-operative, public; never has there been a more intelligent, creative and responsive concept of the role of finance in the building of the community and region.

Bigness in banking has helped bring this to pass, whether the banking is commercial banking, mutual, co-operative or public. An outstanding example of Bigness in private commercial banking in its modern role of aiding in the development of a whole region is afforded by a glance at branch banking.

This form of banking is by no means a novel one confined to the United States; in Canada and Britain, for example, it has long been standard and successful practice. The American talent for large-scale enterprises, and for the control of their abuses, indicates that branch banking has an even greater future in the United States. The best known, oldest and largest example is the Bank of America in the state of California.

California's history, in the past forty years, has been one of extraordinary growth in population and in wealth. In this unique development the diversity of men's ways of making a livelihood and therefore the demands made upon its credit system moves over as wide a spectrum as the diversity of California's climate, from the high Sierras to the Imperial Valley. This has required financing of every conceivable need, from the building of countless homes for a burgeoning population to the requirements of the mining industry, from avocado ranches to tuna canning, from cotton raising (a relatively new crop) to the special needs of an old industry, shipping, from the need for credit for Mickey Mouse and the cartoon movie industry to individual consumer credit for washing machines, from funds for huge metropolitan water systems to small local community paving programs.

Bigness played a determining role in the supply and distribution of credit for a large part of this great story of American development. The largest bank in terms of resources in the United States—seven and a half billions of dollars—is not in "old" New York City but in "new" California, the Bank of America National Trust and Savings Associaton. Within the state the Bank of America has developed the branch bank system to a degree not known elsewhere in the country. The number of branches is impressive; as of September 30, 1952, there were 537 branches throughout California. There is hardly a community so small that one does not find in it a branch of the Bank of America. The sheer number of its deposit accounts— 5,111,524—and the variety of its services, reflect a most intensive use of private banking facilities and a varied utilization of credit as an integral part of the development of California.

16

Bigness and Conservation of Natural Resources

MORE and more of the things we produce or use in our factories and consume in our homes, in addition to food, are made from products of the soil or the forest—plastics, textile fibers, drugs and so on. Therefore anything that undermines and wastes these natural resources threatens us all. On the other hand, whatever serves to make our natural resources go further and endure is in the national interest.

On the basis of my own observation I conclude that today, on the whole, not smallness but size is an aid to conservation. If I am right in this general proposition, then it is a most powerful reason in support of a national climate of accepting and welcoming Bigness, since strengthening our natural resources has in these latter days become almost a matter of life and death for us as a nation.

Take our farms, for example. The size of the average American farm has been steadily increasing until today it is bigger than ever before in United States history. The 1950 census shows that the size of the average farm has increased to 215.3 acres, an increase over 1920 of 42 per cent. The number of farms of 1,000 acres or more rose 73 per cent in that period. At the same time the total area in farms increased by more than 200,000,000 acres. In some regions, Iowa and Kansas, for example, the owner of a 400-acre farm is commonly referred to as a "small farmer"; and an investment of as much as $20,000 in farm machinery by such a farmer is not unusual.

These larger-sized farms—with a marked decrease in farms operated by tenants and sharecroppers—are doing about the most intelligent job of land conservation ever achieved in America. This is due to many factors: better education in conservation methods through public and university leadership, better farm income, more machinery, better roads, farm electricity and so on.

In my opinion, size has contributed in a salutary way in this progress of farm conservation and output. Moreover, I would suppose that, within limits, a further continued increase in the size of American farms—which can be anticipated—will be in the interest of conserving our natural resource of land.

An even more significant contribution to conservation and the best utilization of the land is that of industrial research and production that make possible increased yields of food and fiber for the mounting needs of this nation.

Industrial research in large laboratories (some public institutions, but chiefly those of private industry) and improved production techniques are adding at a rapid rate to the chemical tools by which the farmer can bring new vitality to the land, achieve greater output per acre and man hour of labor, and increase the soil's fertility and security. It is this strength of the soil, in terms of nutrients and composition that is the key to the future conservation of the soil.

New technology, developed jointly by industry, farm organizations and TVA's large chemical facility at Muscle Shoals, holds out the certainty of great improvement in the nourishment of the soil and its wiser use. Basically improved and highly concentrated phosphate fertilizers, and an economical combination of phosphatic and nitrogenous materials, play an important role in this emerging chapter of American agriculture. Industry is now recognizing the need for large integrated fertilizer plants which in time will replace most of the two hundred and more small separate phosphate acidulation plants, and the eight hundred dry mixing plants.

The development of new kinds of weed killers—products of Bigness in research and production—are another contribution of size to better farming. The hand weeding of a cotton field is being replaced by the use of chemical compounds so that what with hand labor takes fifty-four hours per acre can be done by chemicals in five hours. A chemical treatment by plane can do the job of weeding a cornfield in twelve minutes that would require many hours with a cultivator or by a man with a hoe.

The further development of insecticides is another aspect of this same revolution in farming that takes place in research laboratories and industrial plants far removed from the farm itself. A recent example of an advance in this field, one of scores, is the product Systox (produced by a division of Pittsburgh Coke & Chemical Co.), believed to be the forerunner of a new group of insecticides that are picked up by the roots or absorbed by the leaves of a plant.

But the most striking and most recent example of what Bigness in industry can do for conservation of soil is the whole family of soil conditioners announced during 1952 by the Monsanto Chemical Co., the American Cyanamid Co. and others. Monsanto's product, which it calls Krilium, is illustrative. When this chemical agent is applied to the land in small quantities it has the effect, on hard, compact and unworkable soil, of improving its texture and structure, giving it some of the qualities most prized in soil. Moreover, extensive testing by agricultural experiment stations indicate that these soil conditioners minimize destructive soil erosion. They may make it feasible to bring back to life vast acreages that man in his ignorance or heedlessness has rendered sterile, such as the overirrigated and salty "waterlogged" areas of the subcontinent of India and the Middle East.

This is not to say that the laboratory and factory of big enterprise will displace the need for farm families working on their own acres, full of knowledge of the ways of the land and imbued with an almost mystical love of farming as a way of living. These human qualities, it goes without saying, will always be essential, and one may hope will never die. But it seems clear to me that science, and this chemical field in particular—where Bigness is essential—is the new frontier of land conservation and the brightest hope in the world's race against hunger.

As to the forests, the very best demonstrations of conservation practices and management under private ownership in this country are those on huge forest areas owned and run by large, and in some cases very big, businesses. Bigness and prudent, long-view management of our forest resources have, *in recent years,* been demonstrated to be consistent and profitable.

The latter-day operations of the Weyerhaeuser interests, in the Northwest, as one example, show the advantages which size can give in utilizing the skills of professional foresters, chemists and management engineers in making the very best use of our forests and their products in ways not known forty years ago.

The great work of schools of forestry and of the large scientific and technical services of the Federal government —such as the Forest Products Research Laboratory at Madison, Wisconsin—have advanced the science and art of forest conservation. Legislation which years ago was often opposed by large timber interests, forced a new look at the depredation of forests and the long-range economic soundness of scientific forestry. But the actual *application* of such technical knowledge so the forests will contribute to the development of the country is a job primarily for the private owners and operators of forests—in short, for businessmen.

On the whole, the outstanding leadership in forest management on private lands, and research and development for further conservation of wood products, is now to be found among larger business enterprises. This conclusion, based upon my own observation and experience, in the Tennessee Valley and elsewhere, is confirmed by such surveys as that of the President's Material Policy Commission, reporting in June, 1952. In Volume I of this report the

Commission has many interesting things to say about the relative public benefit this nation derives, in a conservation sense, from big as contrasted with small timber holdings and their handling. To conservationists who still hold to the historic view about the evils of Bigness a reading of this document is strongly indicated; it contains such representative expressions as these:

... The situation [as to conservation practices] was best for land held publicly or by large private owners ... the poor management of most small privately owned holdings is the most critical area. ...

The time element appears to be the chief reason for the wide differences. Commercial forest land in public ownership and that owned by large and medium-sized holders is relatively well managed because the owners think in long-range terms. Small holders of forest land often have very different attitudes. [Vol. I, p. 40.]

The application of conservation practices is not limited to the way in which the forests themselves are managed in such vital matters as selective cutting, replanting and fire protection. The more complete utilization of all the "waste" products of sawdust, branches and previously discarded slabs, edgings and veneer pieces has an effect on conservation of the greatest importance. These newer methods are the product of technology.

The recent installation of chippers, as they are called in the Northwest timber region, is an illustration. These machines cut into small particles wood left over from the sawmills and veneer plants; for years these leftovers have been wasted. The chips are then processed into heavy-duty paper and cardboard. In another year or so it is estimated

that 70 per cent of the kraft paper industry in the Northwest will be supplied with raw material from this otherwise wasted wood product. This may reduce the cutting
of lumber by as much as 700,000,000 board feet a year,
saving roughly the equivalent of fourteen square miles of
forest each year.

The industrial use of the forests, for paper and pulp
making, has resulted in pollution of some of the finest
waters in the country. The clear, sparkling mountain
stream that flows past the paper mills near Canton, North
Carolina, is turned to an ugly black when the wastes of
those plants have been dispatched into it; this pollution
affects fish life and human enjoyment of the French Broad
River for many miles of its course.

The pressure of law and public opinion—too long de-
layed—and industry's broader comprehension of the
problem have led to an answer to pollution that will also
be economic. Today industrial research and development
by some of the country's largest paper and pulp companies
are far enough along to assure a double business and community profit. Chemical elements in the wood that were
not previously recovered in the industrial operation of
wood pulp and paper making, but were instead dumped,
as a waste, into the streams of the country have value. If the
processes are sufficiently economical, as now appears, the
business profit of the manufacturers will be enhanced at the
same time the public interest in the *complete* use and conservation of forest products is served. By utilizing these
materials rather than washing them into the streams, another conservation interest will be served, i.e., keeping our
streams clear and unpolluted.

The recent history of the development of our mineral resources tells much the same story of the important and beneficial function of Bigness in making the best use of our minerals, and conserving them.

A simple illustration—one out of scores—is afforded by potash. This essential ingredient in the raising of food is being treated by such a large concern as International Minerals and Chemical Corporation, in its great New Mexico operations, so that not only fertilizer but also other useful substances are produced, such as hydrochloric acid and magnesium oxide.

A complex illustration of the role of Bigness, far too involved for complete exposition here, concerns the oil industry.

For a nation that depends so completely upon petroleum the most rational and orderly development of our oil resources is obviously imperative. We possess great oil reserves, but of course they are not inexhaustible. Moreover, in the vital development of oil in other parts of the world by American oil concerns conservation practices are essential to the protection of our own interests, as well as our good repute in the world.

Conservation of oil requires a conscious, deliberate agreement to relate production to consumption. Whether this is called "planning" or some other term, the result of agreed production must somehow be attained; uninhibited all-out competitive production would insure the most profligate and irresponsible handling of oil reserves. The American people would be the losers thereby, as in the past we have suffered grievous loss by just such irrational competition.

This has all been recognized, as a matter of public oil policy. The Department of Interior and an industry group, the National Petroleum Council, today estimate production, and an Interstate Compact Commission regulates that production.

But oil supply for this country is not a matter confined to the territorial limits of the United States. It is a worldwide matter. The same principles of conservation, by rational production controls to match needs, are required as much on the world scene—perhaps more so—as domestically.

It is therefore puzzling to the average citizen to find that in 1952 several of the principal oil producers of the United States were accused by the government of constituting an illegal international "cartel" because, by an alleged agreement among them in years past, they sought to create some order in the development of world resources of oil, by a kind of production-consumption agreement that has long been recognized as essential. This attack upon these large American oil companies as impairing competition is all the more difficult for the lay observer to understand, in view of the patently furious competitive rivalry between the major oil-refining companies in this country.

It would be strange if as an outcome of this proceeding a dogma of unrestrained competition were to be arbitrarily required and enforced as to the world-wide development of oil resources, when the application of such dogma to the "conservation" of domestic oil supplies has been so universally recognized as wasteful and against the public interest.

PART IV

THE HAZARDS OF BIGNESS

17

New Worries for Old

EUGENE Holman, president of the Standard Oil Company of New Jersey, speaking some time ago about "The Public Responsibilities of Big Companies," expressed the opinion that "most Americans are friendly to big business." Then he went on to say:

But we cannot forget that this country was founded by people who came here to escape tyrannies—things too big for them to handle—the power of the seventeenth- and eighteenth-century state or church, for example. The memory is deeply ingrained. We have never forgotten the lesson—and I hope we never will. The American people keep a wary eye turned toward all forms of bigness. . . . Wherever bigness seems to them to be a danger to the individual, Americans condemn it. And they are quite capable of giving it rough treatment, if necessary.

Mr. Holman is certainly right that it is a good thing for Americans to "keep a wary eye turned toward all forms of bigness," and on all tendencies, in any quarter, to abuse power and use it arbitrarily. This wariness is a sign of health. It is a perennial warning to all those—in business and finance, labor, farming or government—who throw their weight around. Some large utility holding companies ignored this warning in the twenties. Their dismemberment, by law, was an almost inevitable consequence. The people of this country are by no means helpless in the face of abuses by Bigness.

But it is the epitome of reaction to refuse to recognize change. In the light of the profound political and social change that has come over this country during this century, and particularly since the 1930's, the issue I raise is the need for a new viewpoint adapted to the conditions of a new America. But I do *not* say, nor imply, that other potential dangers arising out of new aspects of Bigness do not exist, dangers to competition, to economic freedoms and to our free institutions. They certainly do (in one form or other).

Some of these are quite new. Such a one is the unprecedented *economic* power of the military establishment. The services now constitute, and for a decade or more in the future may continue to be, the most powerful economic force in our entire history: as the greatest purchaser of goods, the chief support and guide of scientific research, the largest claimant on our manpower.

Still another such new possible occasion for future concern, in terms of economic power, is presented by our life insurance companies as a major source of "privately placed" financing for a variety of industrial enterprises. This huge financing function grows out of the unique role of insurance in American life, and the high and deserved confidence in which the companies are held by many millions of policyholders, who trust them with the investment of billions of their savings. But unlike other outside major financing of industry, these huge loans are not subject to

Security and Exchange Commission scrutiny or analogous public regulation. An abuse of this considerable power, or even a series of sizable financing mistakes or improprieties, affecting as it would many people of small means, could be damaging indeed.

Still another new potential problem of economic power inheres in the rise of the industrial pension fund. Their establishment is one of the most reassuring developments of recent years; the handling of these enormous funds, however, is not surrounded with regulatory safeguards analogous to those which experience has confirmed to be wise in the case of other broadly comparable trust functions. Moreover, as these funds increase in magnitude— they have already reached a total in the billions—the fund trustees who invest them not in bonds but in industrial common stocks (which they usually must do to achieve the fund's objectives) will possess what may add up to effective control of some of our very largest industrial corporations.

One further instance of a problem of the abuse of Bigness concerning which there has already been much public discussion and a considerable body of legislation. This is the extraordinary economic power now exercised by the officers of national labor unions. As in the other instances I have just cited, such power has its constructive and beneficial side; it also has its worrisome aspects in the dire consequences upon the entire public of its abuse, or irresponsible exercise.

So we shall continue to face new worries and dangers, potential and operative, revolving about the issue of economic power: its responsible and creative use and its arbitrary and destructive abuse. But we ought to worry about the right things at the right time. This it seems clear to me is not the time to be preoccupied with the *tra‑ditional* dangers of concentrated industrial economic power. The white blood corpuscles in the American blood-stream have shown themselves effective in fighting off ills of this character; the risks are at a minimum at the very time that the advantages of size to the country and to us as individuals are at their greatest.

But the acutely suspicious and fearful mood about Big-ness continues. It is not confined to people of small in-comes nor to those of liberal or labor points of view. The most consistent and emotional critics of Bigness in busi-ness are organizations of small businessmen, one of the most conservative groups in the country. Public figures critical of Bigness often include outstanding conservatives, as is illustrated by the following instance.

In March, 1950 (this was *before* Korea), the Joint Con-gressional Committee on the Economic Report issued a report taking sharp issue over a recent increase in steel prices, and "taking out after" the industry generally. Senator Taft differed with the report in a number of ways. He found no "collusion" among steelmakers, and that competition was "reasonably active." He then considered whether steel prices might not be too high, and "whether the U.S. Steel Corporation is so predominant that it has power to fix prices and at least modify the usual effects of competition"; just what this means was not clear, par-ticularly in the light of the fact that U.S. Steel has a far smaller share of the total steel business now than it did several decades ago. The Senator went on to propose that

Congress "should consider whether we should place a limit on the proportion of any industry which can be controlled by one company."

How seriously Senator Taft intended his far-reaching proposal of a fixed limitation, by law, on how big a steel company might become I do not know. But from a legislator of his considerable standing in the business community, the Senator's suggestion does serve to illustrate the sense of uneasiness about Bigness that in one degree or another pervades most areas of Congress and the Executive Department and of American lay thinking generally.

How can one account for this state of opinion about America's greatest functional asset, size?

There are, I think, five principal causes of this uneasiness—and even fear—five emotions about Bigness, as I have observed them in myself during the past fifteen years; these are much the same sources of concern I observe in others.

First: Big Business threatens us with an increasing concentration of economic power so great as to endanger our very liberties. Big Business has in short become something "too big to handle."

Second: Bigness has brought with it an extreme of centralization; this in turn has produced an unwholesome *centralization* in government ("Big Government") and a corresponding unwholesome centralization in the unions of employees ("Big Labor").

Third: Bigness, far from being efficient, is by its very nature ponderous and bureaucratic, ridden with red tape; it is sterile and orthodox; it lacks mobility, originality and daring.

Fourth: Bigness stifles and suppresses competition, and therefore the system of free enterprise.

I have previously discussed this issue in Part II. I will return to it in Part V, Chapters 21 and 22, which deal more specifically with our antitrust laws, and in which I propose the basis of a new legal policy.

Fifth: Bigness destroys individual independence, and the sense of the individual's own importance. It therefore strikes at the very root of our most cherished political and religious faiths.

This fear I shall comment upon in the concluding chapter of this book.

The succeeding chapters of Part IV are devoted to a discussion of the first three of the hazards or limitations of Big Business listed above.

18

Concentration of Power:
"Too Big to Handle"

THIS is the most commonly held fear of Bigness. Only a people indifferent to their liberties or historically inexperienced in the evils of the concentration of power in a few hands would pass off such a hazard lightly. Americans do not answer this description. The potential danger that inheres in concentration of power is a real issue. It cannot be dismissed as a mere demagogic appeal. It must be dealt with soberly and on its merits.

That business is concentrated in the United States is clear. Bigness—that is, "concentration" in large units—is a prime characteristic of a number of sectors of American industry.

The extent and degree of concentration vary greatly from industry to industry, just as what constitutes a large business varies from industry to industry. What is big in one field—book publishing, or dental supplies, or carpets and rugs—would not be big in chemicals, for example, or primary metals. There is no absolute definition of what is big or what is "concentrated."

Are Bigness and concentration on the increase, or are they stabilizing, or are they on the decline? There is no generally accepted answer. The Federal Trade Commission has recently reported that the trend is rapidly toward greater concentration. President Truman, in signing a recent (1951) amendment to the antitrust laws stated: "During World War II . . . the long-standing tendency toward economic concentration was accelerated." The Democratic party expressed the same idea in the platform adopted in July, 1952; under the heading "Enforcement of Anti-Trust Laws" is the following: "Free competitive enterprise must remain free and competitive if the productive forces of this nation are to remain strong. We are alarmed over the increasing concentration of economic power in the hands of a few."

Whether this increase has actually taken place is the

subject of the widest disagreement among equally well-qualified economists. Certainly in some industries the share of assets or sales in any one concern has markedly declined —such as aluminum or steel or oil; in others the reverse is true. The statistics for the country as a whole, however, are more often than not an inconclusive hodge-podge. At a symposium in June, 1952, on the subject of concentration, the figures submitted by Professor M. A. Adelman of Massachusetts Institute of Technology were discussed and criticized; but Dr. Adelman observed that no disagreement was expressed with the proposition that "since 1931 there has at least been no further concentration."

But whether bigger in relation to the total in any particular industry (or segment of an industry), certainly the size of individual companies has grown enormously, and in Professor Berle's phrase "the unchallenged minimum of facts" establishes concentration as a characteristic in our basic industries.

It must be kept in mind, however, that small business is also a familiar phenomenon, and that the number of very small businesses is huge. In New York City, for example, according to the latest available figures (for 1948), out of 234,540 companies, employing 3,000,000 people, 209,599 employed fewer than twenty people. New York is far from typical, but the figures do suggest the fact that our high degree of concentration has not blotted out a great multiplicity of business enterprises. Twenty years ago if one walked through the great northeast Philadelphia industrial section—one of the greatest in America—he was struck by the diversity in size of industry, with a heavy emphasis on small and specialized manufacturers living next door to the big fellows. Today, as I visit this industrial center, I am impressed by this same fact. A similar condition can be observed in many smaller industrial cities. For example, a count made in 1952 indicated that General Electric's plant in Syracuse, New York, depends upon 669 small firms, in that city alone, for materials and parts for G.E.'s electronic output at that one plant.

The over-all national statistics about the number of business firms appears to bear out the same conclusion: that Big Business is by no means extinguishing small business. The U.S. Department of Commerce reported that at the end of 1950 there were 3,986,000 active businesses in the United States, with a net increase of 33,000 businesses in that year, and a net gain of more than 625,000 concerns since 1940. During 1950 new businesses in the number of 398,000 were started, and 406,000 during 1951. For the first eight months of 1952 Dun & Bradstreet reported 62,104 new incorporations, an increase over the same months of 1951 of 7.7 per cent.

Someone has said that during recent years the big get bigger and the small get smaller. A more accurate statement would be that the big get bigger and the small more numerous.

Bigness is not always a competitive advantage. Small businesses often beat the larger ones in mobility and imagination as well as on costs and quality, and Big Business is forced to try to adjust to this fact. For example, in many specialized types of manufacture it is usually true that massive overhead costs, slower movement or the emphasis on standardized mass production of Big Business puts it at a disadvantage in competition with small companies. Hundreds of illustrations could be cited (though common observation itself confirms the point) wherein small manufacturers excel in the production of their specialty in competition with Big Business. This is simply the other side of the coin that we need Big Business to do the things that require great size, and a further demonstration of the fluidity and flexibility of our competitive economic system.

An interesting instance involves a small concern, American Silver Company of Flushing, Long Island, New York. This concern welcomes orders for manufacturing metal strip rolling of the kind the new jet engine instrumentation requires. Specifications call for thinness of the strips as low as one-half-thousandth of an inch, and tolerances of one-ten-thousandth. Large metal rollers (such as the big steel mills) ordinarily decline such nonstandard specifications, because they are full of headaches for a big mill.

The same proposition is illustrated by the fact that most Big Business secures a major portion of its equipment, components and supplies from quite small concerns, because it is cheaper and more efficient than making these commodities itself. The Standard Oil Company (New Jersey), in 1951, for example, purchased from 26,171 concerns about $400,000,000 of supplies as part of its job of producing, refining and marketing its petroleum products. More than half this total business was done with firms having less than 500 employees. Ninety per cent of United Aircraft Corporation's subcontractors and suppliers are reported in

1952 as having fewer than 500 employees. The Pratt & Whitney division of United Aircraft alone has 5,300 active subcontractors and suppliers. For United as a whole fifty cents out of each dollar it receives is passed on to outside and predominantly small businesses.

Here, as in many other areas, big and small business complement and benefit each other.

Those who are genuinely concerned lest there be a weakening of small business *vis-à-vis* Big Business sometimes *assume* that the public interest has suffered if the figures show that there has been increased concentration in a particular industry, that is, a lesser percentage of the business done by small firms. Some candidates for public office act as if they must make such an assumption, "because there are more small businessmen than big." But surely the rest of us have some duty to point out that, in many situations, an increase in larger firms may be the best thing that could happen for the consumer and the general interests of the community.

There is indeed such a thing as the "curse of bigness," in Justice Brandeis' phrase of a generation ago. But there is also the curse of smallness and it infects large parts of the world.

The low state of health, economic *and political*, resulting from the fragmentation of the European steel industry I have already referred to. I have called attention to the inhumanity of the distribution and credit systems characteristic of the underdeveloped and backward areas of the world, as products of antisocial forms of small business. But the American scene, too, is marked by the curse of

smallness. For example, segments of the lumbering indus‑
try, or some of the low-standard non-union coal-mining
areas, such as those of east Tennessee or west Kentucky,
are typically small-concern operations. It is the bigger coal
companies that are all under collective-bargaining agree‑
ments, with the best safety measures and the most liberal
welfare funds. One could cite other industries of low "con‑
centration" that are also no source of pride. Which is only
to say that to *assume* that small independent business is
always a virtue and "concentration" a synonym for evil
can be quite wrong.

If we are to be honest, we must face the reality that there
may be the soundest technological and humane reasons
why in particular circumstances fewer small businesses
may be a mark of progress rather than the reverse. There
may be simple business reasons as well. The death of a
small business may, upon examination, be simply part of
the process of weeding out the poorly managed concern,
not a sign of manhandling of small business by big.

A society in which no small business can go bankrupt
without thereby raising a political issue and a subsidy to
keep it alive, is certainly not in a healthy state of competi‑
tion, whatever other merits it may have. It is now the
established practice for the government to pay "price dif‑
ferentials to small companies," that is, a higher price than
is paid to big concerns for the same items, where this is
required to keep their facilities available for defense pro‑
duction. I have no basis for doubting that this is a necessary
and wise step, under special circumstances. But the policy
is not confined to defense production or to special cases.

High-cost producers are always able to present reasons why their survival is indispensable, witness the successful sectional, political pressure for "differentials" or just undisguised subsidies to keep high-cost small mines in business, in the Rocky Mountain region. As a matter of social policy, or to encourage some types of mineral development, this may well be worth what it costs—though it is plenty. However justified this may be on other grounds, no one should continue to represent this as a measure designed to keep vigorous and alive the system of "free and competitive enterprise."

As I have said, whether concentration is increasing or decreasing is not clear from the statistics. But what is clear, it seems to me, is that the profound changes that have occurred in our country change the *meaning* to be drawn from such facts as we have. These deep changes should alter our whole outlook on the dangers implicit in the concentration which characterizes basic industry today. And yet much of the discussion of the hazards of concentration too often proceeds on its way as if little had changed since the days of the original passage of Senator Sherman's Antitrust Act, the Oil Trust, the Whiskey Trust, Commodore Vanderbilt, Edward H. Harriman, and others of the long line of those Theodore Roosevelt denounced as "malefactors of great wealth," and Franklin Roosevelt called "economic royalists."

When these old battle cries are sounded today, for the most part they seem theatrical and dated. But this does not mean *new* kinds of dangers arising out of concentration may not be brewing.

Organized labor and organized Big Business, for example, conceivably could form a coalition, leaving the consumer and taxpayer out in the cold. Now and then one sees sporadic evidences of this on particular issues. The bill-poster employee unions and the concerns that erect billboards do at times join hands to fight those who would bar billboards on scenic highways. Unions and power companies with which they have closed-shop contracts sometimes join together in opposing extensions of public power.

Actually this kind of collaboration between employees and employers has been going on for a long time, as to particular issues, such as tariff protection. The recent move to increase the tariff on the importation of watches (denied by President Truman in August, 1952) was pushed vigorously by a coalition of the watch-makers union and the employers in the industry, a reminder of many such special-purpose combines of the days when the tariff was a more familiar issue than it is today.

But the risk seems remote indeed that unions and management will form an alliance against the consumer and the public interest, as a matter of general economic and political strategy.

Still another similarly remote contingency sometimes raised as an objection to Big Business is of quite a different sort; indeed it is at almost the other end of the spectrum. The argument is that Big Business will lead inevitably to "statism," defined as wholesale public ownership of large businesses. The contention is that by breaking up or inhibiting Big Business, we can provide an antidote against this danger of galloping socialism.

Most people apparently have become somewhat skeptical, not to say weary, of the style of economic or political argument which always winds up with the general warning that such and such a course "leads down the road to socialism." Now it is predicted that we must break up Big Business or we are headed down that same road. But we were told the same thing about the income tax, workmen's compensation, the prohibition of child labor, the guarantee of bank deposits and home mortgages, public housing and I know not what else. Despite these forebodings, the fact is that in terms of state ownership of "the means of production and distribution" we are by all odds the least socialistic industrial nation on earth.

The argument that Big Business invites socialism, whereas an economy of smaller business units operates to bar it, rests, I suppose, in large measure upon the thesis that essentially Big Business is monopolistic: that as this becomes more and more evident there will be great public pressure to take these monopolies over as government enterprises, as the only way to protect the consumer and the public. But as the reader knows, this assumption of fact about monopoly conditions is one I assert is contrary to one's everyday observation of the New Competition, described in Part II.

A genuine fear (not just fear-mongering) that Big Business will catapult us into socialism overlooks the saving factor of diversity in the American temperament, and hence in our economy. It overlooks the workings of the

Emersonian "law of compensation" that corrects against extremes. Because a community decides to own its own electric plant does not signify that it will then proceed to own its grain elevators; because a city goes into a public-housing venture does not mean that it is hell bent to take over all housing. This may be "inevitable" to those who are overly logical or overly dogmatic. But in America all kinds of institutions—profit and nonprofit, public and private and co-operative, big and little—function comfortably side by side. We do not feel bound, as a people, to be logical, or ideological, about such matters. We do "what comes naturally." If a method of getting things done, whether it is private or public or co-operative, does not work well, we try some other way. And if it does work, we don't worry too much about some tag that may be put on it.

The same practical talent for diversity and adaptation will protect us from statism through Big Business, in my opinion. Big Business, take it as a whole, is doing a good job; if the viewpoint and policy recommended in this writing were accepted, it could do a far better job for the public interest. If Big Business and the principle of growth are not prevented from functioning at their best, it is inconceivable to me, as a practical matter, that there will be any substantial sentiment that the government take over our major big industries.

Does Big Business impair our liberties and weaken our democracy because, by the use of its huge resources and consequent influence, it can "slant" education and the organs of public information and sentiment in its favor?

Can corporate resources and economic influence be so used as to purchase political power, to a degree dangerous to American liberties?

Fears of this kind on the part of knowledgeable and substantial people—including people who are part of Big Business—have not infrequently been expressed to me. In the past twenty-five years we have seen just enough crude attempts to use contributions to university funds and political campaigns, advertising revenues, benefactions for ministers' retirement, etc., etc., to these ends to know that this worry is not something dreamed up out of the thin air.

Efforts to exercise undue influence—by which I mean *coercion* by money or by influence—have characterized all manner of our institutions and all kinds of people, not Big Business in particular. "Putting on the heat" is neither a monopoly of Big Business, nor of people of wealth. Any experienced public servant knows that pressure (as distinguished from an appeal on the merits) is attempted quite ruthlessly, on occasion, by people with no financial interest at stake whatsoever.

The efforts of the National Electric Light Association in the twenties to "bear down" on the press, tamper with school texts, and throw its weight around in elections, created so violent a public reaction that it is still green in memory after more than twenty years. This episode's sequel was such as not to invite repetition. Though now and then there are isolated efforts to use such tactics, on the whole it seems to me that Big Business has not been guilty of overaggressiveness in presenting its viewpoint and affirmatively espousing its record. If anything, it has erred on the other side, in being too vague and rhetorical, and even negative and defensive. Too often the task of stating its case has been delegated to professional sloganeers rather than assumed by those executives who do the work and therefore know the story at first hand. These limitations have often been pointed out by business' own leadership.

Now it is implicit in what I say in this book that we would all benefit by a better understanding of Big Business and the New Competition; the educational, expository and propaganda efforts of large business, to date, have not been as effective as the overall merits of the case would justify.

Is there, then, solid basis for a fear of undue influence by Big Business on education and the public mind? Such efforts as have been made have certainly not succeeded in any marked way, to put it moderately. There is no sign, so far as my observation extends, that there are elements in the immediate future that will markedly change this picture. But if they should appear, I have not the slightest doubt that the American people would once again take the most drastic action to curb the concentration of industry if they believe it endangers our system of elections or the free and open competition of ideas within our schools, colleges and universities, and in the press and over the airwaves.

19
Centralization and Bigness

THAT Bigness has resulted in centralization is too obvious to require elaboration. Many of the decisions that in the days of smaller enterprise were made in the home-town store or the local factory office now are made at a central point, where the control of the whole system is lodged. Many small and scattered plants have been superseded by a few huge ones.

The degree of such centralization varies, of course, but the proposition stands: Bigness has brought centralization and a degree of remote control to American business. Indeed, it is this very centralization that has brought to the American people many of those advances in productivity, in lowered costs, improved service, shorter hours of labor, to which I have made reference.

Weighed against these obvious advantages, centralization (whether in business or in government) brings with it certain plain and unmistakable evils. But there are decentralizing techniques of administration which, if well conceived and executed, can minimize many such evils, without sacrifice of the benefits of large-scale undertakings.

In the Federal government the hazards of too great

centralization of authority in Washington are quite apparent to the average individual. On this subject, in the course of proposing certain alternatives, I have expressed myself on many occasions. As a public servant I had a part in developing and putting into actual practice methods of decentralization of the national governmental powers lodged in the TVA, and in the Atomic Energy Commission's undertakings. As representative of my views, I quote from a book written in 1943:

Centralization in administration promotes remote and absentee control, and thereby increasingly denies to the individual the opportunity to make decisions and to carry those responsibilities by which human personality is nourished and developed.

I find it impossible to comprehend how democracy can be a living reality if people are remote from their government and in their daily lives are not made a part of it, or if the control and direction of making a living—industry, farming, the distribution of goods—is far removed from the stream of life and from the local community.

It is folly to forget that the same dangers and the same temptations exist whether the centralization is in government or in mammoth business enterprises. In both cases the problem is to capture the advantages that come with such centralized authority as we find we must have, and at the same time to avoid the hazards of overcentralized *administration* of those central powers.

It can be done. It can be done in many business operations as well as in government activities.*

Much of the book from which the above excerpts are quoted is devoted to a description of the principles of de-

---

* *TVA: Democracy on the March.* Harper & Brothers, 1944, pp. 139, 142.

centralization in government in which I believe, and to illustrations of how these principles have been put to practical use. With modification, these principles are applicable to large business enterprises. And of course many businesses have long used analogous techniques of decentralized management. Others are in process of working out such methods, tailored to their particular problems.

The central principle I espouse is that we make a firm working distinction between centralized decisions of *policies* affecting the whole huge enterprise and the decentralized or delegated *execution* of those policies.

Vital—and inevitable—as further decentralization in business administration certainly is, one must concede that the evil consequences of business overcentralization are not of the same gravity as are the hazards inherent in overcentralization in government.

The reason, of course, lies chiefly in the difference in the relation of the individual to sovereign government, and to private competitive business (legal private monopolies, such as utilities and carriers, stand on another footing). If the overcentralized operation of a huge private business produces very bad results, the management will ordinarily be compelled to do something about it, and often rather promptly. Customers will complain. Suppliers or bulk buyers will make their views known, or go elsewhere. Competitors will not be slow to take advantage of the situation. Labor unions, under collective bargaining procedures, will present the employees' complaints. And so on. But in government (where, unfortunately, collective bargaining is a rarity), and in the case of legal monopolies, all of these correctives of competition do not exist; and alternative correctives are relatively slow in securing day-to-day improvements.

There is an even more vital distinction. The blight of overcentralized administration is in its deadening effect on *individuals*. In business, this is serious enough for its employees, certainly. But in government the effect of overcentralization is felt not only in the dullness and sterility of the working life of its employees. The consequences go deeper still, weakening the very foundations of our system of political freedom. For overconcentration at the nation's capital, distant from the everyday life of ordinary people, serves to deaden their sense of participation and partnership in government affairs. This citizen participation is at the heart of our concept of democracy.

Though the consequences of business overcentralization upon the individual—the worker, or manager of big enterprise, or the customer—may not be as grave as in government, they are serious. To a large degree they are preventable by the adoption of specific management policies and methods. More and more, industrial management is coming to see that the job of a great industry is not only to produce a good product at a profit, but to develop people; that people do not develop and grow unless they are given responsibility, either as individuals or as members of groups; that in overcentralized operations men are denied real responsibility, except at the center; that decentralization is not genuine unless, in the language of the new president of General Electric, "we envision . . . actual authority for making decisions . . . at points as near as possible to where actions take place."*

Moreover, the integration of a unit of a huge nationwide enterprise *into the life of the local community* is now coming to be recognized as an essential of sound big management. With such a large business as the Bell System this has been the policy and practice for decades: others, such as the larger merchandizing chains, have made great headway in this direction only in more recent years. This principle affects the kind of men Big Business selects to head its *regional* or *local* plant or store, the increased independence of decision given them, their status in the organization, whether they are mere rubber stamps for the central office or representatives of the business in their own right.

Decentralization in business can take many forms. Geographic dispersion of its plants and contracting for the special skills of independent small manufacturers and suppliers, while quite different, are both examples of decentralization. Dividing the business up along functional lines, or on a regional basis, or emphasizing internal competition by the various methods available are other manifestations of the same salutary principle.

There is nothing in the constants of the nature of Big Business that prevents its effective decentralization. And the pay-off for the business, for the employees, for customers and for communities can be very great indeed.

* Ralph J. Cordiner, "Problems of Management in a Large Decentralized Organization," American Management Association, General Management Series No. 159 (1952).

20

Too Big: The Dangers of Inefficiency, Sterility and Bureaucracy

THERE are those who will agree that size is indeed a great asset, but they are convinced that many businesses have become so huge in magnitude and ramifications that the advantages of size are outweighed by ponderousness, slowness of action and a sterile and bureaucratic spirit. The results such giants have achieved, these critics assert, are due to sheer weight and power, rather than to any of the productive and creative qualities that "sensible Bigness" admittedly affords. Their view is that like the mastodon, which became extinct because it was too big, super-big organizations sin against nature's laws of survival, and are similarly doomed.

These critics (among them conscientious and self-critical employees and executives of such giants) point to the unbelievable slowness with which decisions are ground out of the wheels within wheels that characterize some very large institutions of business. The "medium-sized" corporation, they say, is the most effective for mobility, daring, quick decisions and above all for enterprise and "get-up-and-git."

The youthful head of a new and growing frozen fruit-juice concentrate business, John M. Fox of Minute Maid Corporation, recently described posts in large, long-established businesses as "fur-lined foxholes," in which more and more of our most promising young scientists and executives take cover, for reasons of personal security, because new business is not made more attractive to them. Their talents for innovation might be more usefully employed in new businesses, he thought, and predicted that this trend might produce an "economic dust bowl" in our country.

Viewing Big Business as a natural and a healthy development, the critics of super-bigness point to what they believe is an absence within such huge empires of genuine self-criticism, the lack of a kind of loyal opposition. Whereas, in an earlier period, some family interest or bank was a large owner with an interest in severely holding management to the best performance, now ownership is so diffused that management is largely self-perpetuating, able to solicit proxies that insure its tenure. As a consequence—so the argument runs—these "inside cliques" indulge in self-praise, and put a premium on conformity. The expansion of these giants into new fields or to get more business, it is argued, has only a secondary relation to the increased profitability of the concern; it is often the same kind of "empire building," to increase management's prestige and massage its vanity, that one not infrequently finds and criticizes in bureau chiefs of the Federal government.

Moreover—heavy as are the burdens in any active busi-

ness these days—in super-bigness the load of work that
falls upon the head officers and the second and third
echelon is too great to be borne. It is argued, with great
force, that there are no men strong enough, wise enough
or big enough, to do a *good* job of administering billion-
dollar undertakings; all that the devices of decentralized
management achieve is to make figureheads and public
fronts of the top executives. Geographic distribution and
decentralization of plants make these men the slaves of
airplanes and trains, on the days when they are not chained
to the telephone. The marked increase in public, labor and
governmental relations responsibilities of Big Business
multiplies the amount of time the top men find it necessary
to give to speeches, to dedicating new plants, to top-brass
inspections, etc., all over the country, with frequent business trips to Washington. Add it all up, the argument goes,
and the time has come to recognize that if for no other
reason than the inherent limitations of energy and wisdom
of individual human beings, the super-big company is on
its way out. It should be replaced not by fragmentation
into small business, but divided into companies that represent a moderate and sensible Bigness.

I certainly agree that such criticisms have considerable
basis in the case of some very large enterprises. Many
(though not all) of the advantages of Big Business can
probably be equally well achieved without going to
extremes of size; greater efficiency, liveliness and speed of
action are attainable where Bigness is not extreme.

The argument that a top management can fasten itself
on a super-big concern, with inadequate opportunity for

informed criticism from the outside shareholder, finds plenty of supporting evidence. It is well known that there are some choice stuffed shirts and glorified mediocrities among the upper reaches of our largest organizations. But recent history also shows that however fortified with public relations men and proxy solicitors, when the earnings fall off without good cause, or the company's prestige suffers, getting rid of hollow management is not too difficult or long in the doing.

The heart of the matter is that (except in cases of gross abuse) a *legislative* cure of too-bigness is more dangerous than the disease. For if, in the asserted interest of such factors as efficiency and industrial mobility, we put a legal upper limit on Bigness, then Congress or a commission (as some have proposed) must decide this question: How big is too big?

How can anyone decide that question about a competitive industry or business in a relatively free market without the most profound and restrictive consequences to our fluid economic system? It seems to me that we have no realistic alternative except to leave the verdict to customer acceptance, to the practical test of figures recorded on financial statements, to the success or failure of research programs, to the ability of an enterprise to attract and hold able people, to work out its public relations and its labor relations successfully—in short, to the pragmatic give-and-take of results.

How big a business can be, and still maintain its maximum of innovation, efficiency and liveliness, is not something that can be precisely determined, or generalized about. For example, current new developments in the continuous casting of steel (carried on by Republic Steel Company and the Babcock & Wilcox Company) could conceivably dictate that even such a characteristically Bigness-industry as steel may, in twenty-five years, be more efficient with a multitude of medium-sized corporations than with a relatively few very large ones.

On the other hand, some of the human factors that now put a limit on how big an enterprise can be and still be manageable may yield to some new technical development, such as electronic business machines and similar revolutionary devices.

I have had responsibility for one multibillion-dollar industrial and scientific enterprise and another close to the billion mark. I have had business dealings with most of our super-big companies. From this experience I have come to respect the view that such colossal undertakings often do suffer, from a management point of view, from a lack of compactness and mobility. Many experienced managers would have a similar reaction.

But often I have found that disadvantages of this character, in particular circumstances, are completely and totally outweighed by other factors that require very great size.

In these days operating efficiency is not always as important as the marshaling in one huge enterprise of the funds and diverse minds required for the intricate technological problems our national security and prosperity demand. In other words efficiency, in the accounting and financial sense, may be less important than the unique capacity of very great size to accomplish technical tasks *not possible at all* except on a grand scale.

There is solid reason for believing that the limitations of Bigness will be best corrected through the therapeutic effect of our extraordinarily sensitive and adjustable economic system. The impersonal pressures of the most competitive period in American economic history remain the best protection we have that when mammoth enterprises have lost their special usefulness, they will be forced to yield their place to institutions of a more serviceable size.

In the past we have made progress by applying specific remedies to correct for the failure of Bigness to measure up to the results expected of it by customers, workers, investors, the community generally. Our efforts have not been equally successful when we relied too heavily upon our ability to read the future, by seeking to avert anticipated ills.

It requires more foresight than men are ordinarily blessed with to decide *today* what is too big for *tomorrow*. Tomorrow some scientist in a laboratory, or some quick change in public taste, will render that legislative conclusion either nonsense or unnecessary. The Big Five meat packers in the early twenties were judicially forbidden to compete with the wholesale grocers; this was intended to preserve the wholesalers as an economic institution. This consent decree had no significant effect. The wholesale grocer, in some sections of the country, was doomed, and has pretty well passed out of the picture because of economic forces having nothing to do with meat packing or the Big Five or the antitrust laws. It was, incidentally, largely these same economic forces that made such institutions as the A & P grocery chain inevitable.

A considerable humility about one's ability to foretell

just what technical achievements are possible, or even likely, is an essential of good judgment in these modern times. The fiasco of the Federal Communication Commission's decision effectively giving a legal monopoly to the Columbia Broadcasting Company's system of color television, is a recent case in point.

The Commission-approved C.B.S. color television system was one in which the images broadcast in color could not be received in black-and-white, on existing television sets in millions of homes; that is, the C.B.S. color system was "incompatible" with existing black-and-white receivers. The Radio Corporation of America urged that its system should be preferred because its color broadcasts could be received on existing sets, in high-quality monochrome, without added expense to these millions of set owners; moreover it had the asserted advantage of being all-electronic rather than mechanical as was the C.B.S. system.

The Commission reached its decision on this matter after nine months of hearings on technical aspects of electronics, colorimetry, and other abstruse scientific matters. It made a scientific judgment that a satisfactory all-electronic and compatible color television was not likely of early attainment. The R.C.A. appealed the order to the Supreme Court of the United States. That Court held that it was bound by the conclusions of the "expert" F.C.C. And while this "decision" about the limitations of human ingenuity was still fresh, the scientists in the electronic laboratories were in process of disproving the Commission's thesis. The skepticism of more than one member of the

Court about this legalistic method of deciding scientific issues was expressed for them by Mr. Justice Frankfurter in a separate opinion, *dubiante*, in the course of which he used the following words:

> Experience has made it axiomatic to eschew dogmatism in predicting the impossibility of important developments in the realms of science and technology. Especially when the incentive is great, invention can rapidly upset prevailing opinions of feasibility. . . . One need not have the insight of a great scientific investigator, nor the rashness of the untutored to be confident that the prognostications now made in regard to the feasibility of a "compatible" color television system will be falsified in the very near future.*

Similarly about size. For any body of men to decide that a company of a particular size is too big to be efficient is to make a judgment deeply affected by changing technical developments; overnight it might well prove to be patent and injurious nonsense.

The only practical measure we now have of how big is too big is one that is *after* the fact, i.e., the test of experience: How does this particular size work out, in practice? And it is upon this pragmatic test of "works" that our concern should be concentrated, rather than in abstract and dogmatic condemnation of size as such.

* Radio Corporation of America v. Federal Communications Commission, 341 U.S. 412, 427, 1951.

PART V

A NEW POLICY TOWARD BIGNESS: FROM NO TO YES

21

Trust Busting: Does It Make Sense Today?

T HIS book is not about the antitrust laws. It is concerned with the realities and the potentialities of Big Business, as a social institution clothed with the broadest of functions and responsibilities.

But no discussion of Bigness can ignore the antitrust laws. For the essential fact is that as these laws are now construed, the very Bigness upon which we all now depend may be illegal.

Put thus candidly and plainly, this is slightly insane. It implies, quite correctly, that a shadow of criminality hangs over some of our highly respected business leaders. It suggests, accurately enough, that many obviously beneficial institutions of business whose products we use every day and in which millions of Americans are shareholders await their turn before the bar of justice. This so offends common sense that it has been necessary to envelop the whole subject of the antitrust laws in a fog of legal scholasticism, verbal distinctions without a distinction, economic gobbledygook and regulatory voodoo. So that while one cannot ignore the antitrust laws if he would try to understand the place of Bigness today, his prospect of laying hold of the real issues is almost nil once he tries to follow the abstract meanderings of this labyrinth of antitrust laws and regulations, and their interpretation and the interpretation of the interpretation.

What then are the essential and living issues that need concern those outside the circle of those expert in the lore of trust busting?

The basic and the ultimate issue, I submit, is not whether Bigness is or is not contrary to the Sherman and Clayton acts, as those laws have been judicially construed, nor even whether Bigness impairs competition, as competition was conceived when those laws were enacted many years ago.

The real question for us is whether on the whole Bigness is in the public interest; in other words, are we, the American people, better off for Bigness? If we are—as I believe— and the only possible construction of the Sherman Act makes this illegal, then the comment of a great liberal judge, Mr. Justice Holmes, seems justified that "the Sherman Act is a humbug based on economic ignorance and incompetence. . . ."*

The antitrust laws were enacted many years ago to make us better off by means that then seemed wise and appropriate—as they indeed proved to be. They ought to be construed to achieve that purpose, as I believe they can. But if they cannot be so construed, they should certainly be superseded by laws that do further our best interest, rather than cripple and retard it.

* *Holmes-Pollock Letters.* Harvard University Press, 1941, Vol. 1, p. 163.

When I say the ultimate issue is whether we are "better off" for Bigness, what do I mean by "better off"? I do not mean solely in a material or economic sense—though that is certainly part of it. I mean better off also in the nonmaterial sense, better able to develop the values in life that seem to us important, better off as a nation confronted with great dangers to our security and our very lives, better able to develop the kind of country we deeply desire this land of ours to be.

In our efforts toward this end, the antitrust laws have a profound influence, in two quite different ways.

In the *first* place, those charged with the administration of these laws (the Antitrust Division of the Department of Justice, and the members and staff of the Federal Trade Commission) constitute a kind of F.B.I. of the world of business competition, with a responsibility to detect and to protect the public against acts of coercion, deceit, boycott, collusion or forms of business violence that inflict injury on competitors and the consuming public. Agreements to limit production, or fix prices, to allocate or divide markets, to suppress innovation, to exert economic pressure or to engage in a boycott to keep newcomers from entering into competition—these are among the many courses of conduct over which these public servants have for years exercised a policeman's function, and a highly salutary one.

But in more recent years a second concept of what the antitrust laws mean has arisen, an interpretation mischievous and injurious and unrealistic. This concerns itself not with maintaining competition so much as with who does the competing. If competitors are few in number and big, this is *presumed* to endanger competition, no matter how competitive in fact the situation actually is. In its practical consequences this second doctrine is one of condemnation of concentration, of Bigness, *as such*.

A few paragraphs will suffice, for our present purposes, with respect to the first, or policing function.

The methods and tactics by which business concerns try to stifle competition and injure competitors are about as varied and numerous as any other form of skulduggery. Some of these schemes are rough stuff, about as subtle as a bludgeon; such were the methods, in earlier days. More recently the acts of gouging and coercion are likely to be more complex, and sometimes indirect. But whatever the varied shapes and forms these acts against competition may assume, their effect is much the same: to injure and weaken competition, whether by suppression, coercion, deceit, boycott or other kinds of economic conduct.

The work of the Antitrust Division of the Department of Justice and of the Federal Trade Commission in prosecuting these and similar tangible acts against competition —or combinations to commit such acts—has contributed to the business health of the country. No one, I suppose— *least of all* leaders in business—would propose any weakening of the Sherman or Clayton acts in these policing areas, where so much good work has been done, and so much offside play been inhibited by the very fact that the antitrust laws existed. Certainly, I make no such proposal. On the contrary it is my view that the enforcing officers should concentrate on these specific policing functions, which should be maintained and even strengthened in their administration.

If a Big Business prevents or impedes others from entering its fields of business by coercive or collusive measures, rather than by its economic or technological superiority, it is engaged in stifling competition in plain violation of law. Here is something tangible, concrete, specific. The defendant business has an opportunity to know just what it is charged with.

But as respects the attacks that center on who does the competing, that is attacks on size, *in and of itself,* an entirely different picture is presented. Under the newer doctrine of trust busting, as it exists today, the corporate misdeed of being big need not relate to anything the Big Business has done, or plans or threatens to do. It is not necessary for the government to show that by reason of its size the defendant company in fact *exercise*s a power in a manner that excludes competitors. It is enough that by reason of its size it possesses a power which *if* exercised could exclude competitors; because of its size it is presumed to be a "*potential*" law-breaker, even though it be admitted that it has never taken any step, alone or with a combination, to make use of the asserted power, nor committed any acts of competitive violence, coercion, deceit or collusion. The heart of the offense is the *potential* power to do wrong, not the misdeed itself.

Under this current antitrust doctrine it appears to be no defense against a charge of potential monopoly to show that competition *in fact* exists, in lively fashion, among a score of concerns in the industry. It is equally irrelevant that the Big Business' prices are not unreasonable; that its production has met demands as to quantity and steadily

improved quality and variety; that its technological progress has been outstanding, and that new competitors have
entered the field. It is irrelevant that the defendant Big
Business has been a pillar of the national defense; that its
labor relations and pension funds and welfare plans are
among the best in the industry. It is irrelevant that when
given a free choice customers, by their orders, show confidence in the company's products, prices, service and
reliability, that small businesses have found in the company
a growing market for their own products, that the company
has made its know-how and its own patented inventions
widely available to its competitors, big and small, at reasonable license fees. It is irrelevant that its size has made
possible technological advances that have created a new
industry, and that these inventions have widened the area
of choice and enriched the lives of millions of Americans.

It has been repeatedly said by responsible public servants
that our current antitrust policy is not against Bigness as
such. ". . . size is not the offense" wrote the then head of
the Antitrust Division in January, 1950. "The offense is
the monopoly power or the restraint of trade, the achievement of which was aided by the defendant's size." But then
he states, that

> Unlike the early days of the Sherman Act monopoly power
> is today more likely to be present in an industry in which
> there is a Big Three or Big Four. . . . In determining the
> existence of monopoly power relative position in the industry
> is an important consideration . . . while size in and of itself is
> not a standard for determining monopoly power, in the com-
> parative sense it may well become a serious factor. . . . *

* Herbert A. Bergson, *Bigness in Business*, New York Bar Association,
January 25, 1950.

Such statements, while doubtless sincere, are disingenuous and at odds with the realities. More candid and forthright is the explicit statement of this doctrine that great size is contrary to the Sherman Act formulated by Mr. Justice Douglas.

Size in steel [which was the industry in question] is the measure of the power of a handful of men over our economy. That power can be utilized with lightning speed. It can be benign or it can be dangerous. The philosophy of the Sherman Act is that it should not exist. . . . Industrial power should be decentralized. It should be scattered into many hands so that the fortunes of the people will not be dependent on the whim or caprice, the political prejudices, the emotional stability of a few self-appointed men. The fact that they are not vicious men but respectable and social-minded is irrelevant. That is the philosophy and the command of the Sherman Act.*

The thread that runs through this latter-day doctrine of antitrust is that a few big rivals in an industry present, presumptively, the picture of monopoly, not competition, that size, as the Supreme Court recently put it, is the "earmark of monopoly power." It is the small number and the great size of the companies in an industry, and not the state of actual competition that, in major antitrust proceedings, has been taken as the basis for the presumption that monopoly power exists. I submit that a policy which holds that size is an earmark of monopoly power, and which requires, to establish illegality, only *potential* danger of monopoly due to the existence of power (and not its exercise) is certainly a policy against Bigness per se.

Nor is it any justification to say, as some public servants

* Dissenting opinion in United States v. Columbia Steel Co. 334 U.S. 495, 537.

do occasionally: "If the laws are wrong, they ought to be amended or repealed, but until they are it is our duty to enforce them." It is untenable to say that the broad provisions of basic policy in the antitrust laws can bear no other reasonable construction than that now being put upon them, a construction so at variance with the public interest.

The concept of "potential" wrongdoing is a vague and slippery one; now and then an effort is made to extend it beyond the field of trust busting, into the area of education. Senator Hickenlooper of Iowa, for example, made such a proposal in connection with the selection of recipients of Atomic Energy Commission fellowships for research in non-secret areas of medical and other science. In the future, in choosing these fellows, the National Research Council, he argued, should not only continue to pass on their scholarly qualifications and their moral character, but the Council should also determine whether these students "are subversive in their views, or *reasonably potentially subversive in their views.*"*

This proposal has not, thus far, made any apparent headway among the Senator's colleagues. Nor does it commend itself, in a country of justice under law either on "loyalty" issues or issues respecting Big Business. For under such a doctrine of civil rights or antitrust law no tangible proofs are required in order to arrive at a "decision," which is indeed a great convenience for an official who has prejudged a case, whether on the subject of loyalty or monopoly.

Most of the charges that the very existence of Bigness

* Hearings, Joint Committee on Atomic Energy, 81st Cong., 1st session, p. 62, 1949. See also p. 45.

itself creates monopoly power, or "potential" monopoly, come not from the consuming public but from smaller competitors. Their complaint often is not that Bigness results in too little competition but too much, and of the wrong kind; that the inherent advantages of Bigness (large-scale purchasing, for example, or large-scale and costly research by which valuable patented processes are created) enable the big concern to take a large proportion of the customers, who, of course, prefer the best and the least costly products.

It would throw a great deal of light upon these issues, so far as consumers are concerned, if the Antitrust Division followed a practice of making public the names of the private companies and individuals and the public officials, including Congressmen, upon whose initiative the major antitrust investigations and proceedings were instituted. With the full historical background the public would thus be better able to judge whether the protection of some private interest is the dominant consideration in particular actions against Bigness, and whether that special private interest coincides with the broad public interest.

For the antitrust agencies of government to seek to punish the successful competitor—acts of coercion or collusion aside— *in the name of competition* is difficult for me to comprehend. Nevertheless, this is what we have been witnessing in recent years where success in securing a large proportion of the market or alertness "progressively to embrace each new opportunity as it opened"* is condemned by the courts as "potential monopoly," and hence

* United States v. Aluminum Co. of America 148 F. 2d 416 (1945) quoted with approval in American Tobacco Co. v. United States 328 U.S. 781 (1946).

lawbreaking. To construe the once invigorating Sherman Antitrust Act in this way is to rob it of its great purpose as a stimulant to enterprise and innovation.

However costly it is from the consumer's point of view, however much it holds back the full productive and distributive genius of the country (as I believe it does directly and by indirection), it continues to be the doctrine of our antitrust administration and Congressional policy that if one or several corporations have a big share of the business in their industry, *by that very fact alone* they are "potential monopolists," to be dealt with by cutting them down to size or forcing them to relinquish their advantage or even actively to help their competitors, on pain of severe legal penalties. The need for a realistic re-examination of such a policy seems to me urgent, in the public interest.

The doctrine of penalizing, prosecuting, hectoring and even dismembering a large business which, by research and managerial superiority, achieves competitive success (that is, wins a large share of the market) has serious consequences of a practical kind. It creates some incentive for large and efficient and research-minded concerns not to forge ahead, but to put on the brakes. Further research and improvements would cut costs even more. Aggressive research and sales effort would secure an even larger part of the available market. These steps, beneficial to the company and the country, would or might bring an antitrust action instituted by those charged with protection and furthering of competition!

Thus we consumers must sometimes buy from less efficient producers or retailers, at higher prices, and receive fewer benefits of research, because genuine competition would attract too many customers to the concerns that are the best (from the consumers' point of view) in the industry.

For the courts to chop Du Pont, for example, into several smaller companies, because it is too big, might be to waste the asset of Du Pont's size, one of proved usefulness to the country. (If the present trend of public opinion and of law continues one must expect just this to happen.) Any transgressions of a specific character, whether overt acts against competitors, or acts of suppression that impair competition can be and should be policed and punished. But certainly the continued steady growth of other aggressive and progressive concerns—of which there are many in the chemical field with newcomers being steadily added— affords considerably more assurance of competition than surgical operations performed by the Sherman Act upon the body of Du Pont.

Such considerations as these will be relevant when the time comes for the government to dispose of its very large interests in the war-born synthetic rubber industry. Making quite large rubber industry units out of medium-sized ones may prove a more sensible way to strengthen competition than to dispose of the government plants only to many relatively small concerns.

Do I mean that it is better, for the maintenance of competition, to have only two or three very big concerns of comparable size, a fight among giants, than a score or two of more moderate-sized corporations and their affiliates? There is no universal rule. Certainly it is an oversimplification to measure the vigor and health of competition solely by the relative size of the gladiators in the arena.

But in an industry where it is clear that the position of one or several Big Businesses has, *in fact* (not "potentially" but actually), been so used as to diminish competition among them, then we ought to permit without question the consolidation and merger of smaller companies into larger units even though they were previously competitors, for the over-all effect is to strengthen competition. In other words, for Company A to merge or consolidate with Companies B, C and D, its present competitors, in order better to compete with the industry's giants may, in particular cases, be in the interest of modern competition.

Big Business, in my opinion, has benefited the country; but as I have often pointed out in this writing, it also has its seamy side. Like all human institutions its conduct can rise no higher in the scale of values than the standards of the men and women who make it up. Moreover, under the best of management, the top executives do not exercise day-to-day control and usually can have little detailed knowledge of what goes on in the dealings between their minor executives or sales representatives and those from whom they buy supplies, or to whom they sell their products. However salutary a company's policies, in carrying them out many instances will occur of coercion and pressure, instances of inadequate people throwing their weight around, relying not upon their ability but upon the prestige of their company.

But we should not predicate our antitrust policies and therefore our whole national policy toward Bigness upon the fact that such ugly things do occur. Here is where the policeman's function comes in. If the structure of our Federal government were determined solely by the fact that individual public servants, high or low, occasionally fall from the high standards expected of them, modern government would not exist.

In considering whether our antitrust laws as applied to Bigness per se make sense today, one must not only consider whether these policies are compatible with our best over-all interests. We must also ask: Are there *better ways* than antitrust laws and proceedings to secure and to maintain the kind of economic system we want?

Clearly, there are. During the past twenty years by a combination of government and private action, the nature and scope of the responsibility of Big Business to the whole community has been changed, *with this very public-welfare objective in view*. However imperfectly achieved, we have today a society in which the claims of the whole community upon business have been asserted, and are to a heartening degree being met. The results are extraordinarily good, not only in terms of competition—the sole criterion of trust busting—but by far broader and more meaningful tests, tests that encompass many of the elements of what we conceive to be a good society.

And so, in considering how useful the antitrust laws still are today, it is distinctly relevant that an *alternative* exists, an alternative much more flexible, less legalistic, more comprehensive, and more generally acceptable, and certainly far more effective. The time has come when the general public has a right to ask why these changes in the responsibilities of business to the whole community do not substantially relegate antitrust laws to the role of protection for us against specific acts violative of competition.

Accepting the asserted objectives of antitrust suits against Bigness *per se*, how effective can such suits be? One must admit: not very. This is for the quite simple reason that in the nature of things trust busters *can only act negatively*. They can have certain acts declared illegal and forbidden. They can restrain a company from entering some line of business, or force it to get out of that business by divesting itself of its properties. But there is no effective way the decree in an antitrust proceeding against Bigness can assuredly *affirmatively promote competition* (whether the decree is entered after litigation, or "consented" to by an agreement). To create competition in the world of fact requires the skills and comprehension of management, the resourcefulness of men in laboratories, the ingenuity of salesmen, the confidence of investors. No court order can create these; they are the consequence of affirmative acts of will by individuals.

The extent to which trust busting against bigness, in our now infinitely complex technical society, has become unreal and ineffective to promote the public interest can be seen in still another way, that is by noting the remedies the courts apply to the asserted evils or potential evils of size. For the court decrees are often nothing less than a reconstitution of the whole structure of an entire industry, or a determination that the public interest in competition is served if the Big Business defendant is permitted to do no more than, say, 30 per cent of the business of the industry. This is true whether the remedy is by what is called a "consent decree" (the defendant company agreeing to the decree as an alternative to going through the processes of a long trial) or after an adjudication in court. Such conclusions often represent feats of economic planning that presuppose a knowledge of present and future technology, general economic trends, the reaction of the capital markets today and tomorrow, the sales appeal of various products now and in the future—and a series of conclusions that are plainly beyond the powers of imagination or competence of any judge, or any other public servant, as they are clearly beyond the capacity of any industrial executive except on the basis of particular issues as they arise from day to day or year to year.

22

A Proposal: A Basic Economic Law

MANY of the difficulties about the application of the antitrust laws to Bigness arise, as I have indicated, because the present interpretation of those laws takes *a narrow view of the public interest,* a view so narrow as to be injurious rather than helpful to our country. The objective of the antitrust laws relates to *competition*. The concern of most opponents of Bigness is with *competitors*. The objective of the American people as a whole is neither competition nor competitors. Our goal is far more comprehensive and sensible, to wit to have a certain kind of country in which to live. It is on this basis that I suggest the approach to a change in our laws governing Big Business.

What kind of country is it we want?

As I see it, the kind of America we want to live in, the kind of human society we want for ourselves (and hope might appeal to the rest of the world), has certain *functional characteristics* among which one would include some or all of the following:

A *fluid, changing, enterprising* kind of society. We want to live in a country that is not static and "set in its ways."

We like "newness"; new products, new gadgets, new entries in the competition for our dollars or our favor.

We want to keep it possible—even inevitable—that, no matter how far down the line you start, you (or someone like you) can end on top, and get there not because of caste or status or inherited wealth or orthodox views, but because you excel in your line, whatever it is. We want no rigidity or inflexibility in our society, either socially or physically.

The monumental emphasis our industrial system, our government and our universities now place upon research and development is one important manifestation of this desire for a fluid, changing society, with new kinds of products, but, even more significant, with new kinds of individual opportunities and new and clearer understanding of the physical world.

An *increasingly productive* society: one in which our needs as individuals are met as they appear and as they constantly expand; in which our national needs for military security or for internal public works can be met and steadily expanded. We are not satisfied with "too little" and we are critical of "too late."

An *efficient* and a "speedy" society. We set great store by efficiency and speed; we regard inefficiency and slowness as marks of inferiority. We are "cost conscious." To establish that one course is faster or more efficient than another, or that it cuts cost, is a consideration that weighs heavily with us.

A *diverse* society; one in which there are always many different ways of doing things. We want room for big and small business (regarding both as indispensable, and one complementary to the other); for public and private ownership; for corporations and co-operatives; for profit and nonprofit enterprise—all functioning alongside one another.

We want a *rational* and *stable* economic and social system in that it looks ahead and hence *conserves* its resources. We strongly desire both stability and security. We want the security of keeping our cake, the fun of eating it, and the excitement of having a new and different cake for every meal.

We want a society in which all our institutions are *responsive to the public interest and the public will*.

We want an economic and social system that is *humane* and *fair*; an *ethical* society.

When we think of how we want our country to function, there are two other (and closely related) tests we customarily apply:

To what extent do our policies and our institutions (business included) nourish opportunity for the development of the *individual,* as distinct from their effect upon the community as a whole? To what extent do our policies further our *national security,* by protecting, defending and strengthening the freedom and the liberties of people of the United States of America against dangers—from within and from without?

Such inclusive and fundamental criteria as these suggest an approach to the change I propose in our laws governing Big Business. It will be said that the change I seek could be effected without new legislation, simply by a different judicial and administrative interpretation of the Sherman and Clayton laws. To this I would be inclined to agree. All that would be essential would be to construe the antitrust laws in the context of the whole fabric of facts about Bigness and the public interest to which I have called the reader's attention in this book.

Such a yardstick for measuring Bigness under the antitrust laws would invoke the judicial doctrine that all the surrounding facts and circumstances should be considered, a doctrine advanced by some of our greatest judges, notably Hughes, Brandeis, Holmes and Roberts. It would once more give vitality to the now almost moribund "rule of reason" in construing those laws.

But I see scant prospect that the courts, the staff of the Antitrust Division or the Federal Trade Commission, without years of delay, will return to this earlier and, I think, sounder viewpoint. To wait for perhaps ten years while this change slowly evolves is to lose a great opportunity for accelerated economic progress. I therefore suggest that we seek to make the change through Congressional action on a broad front, a change going far beyond the antitrust laws to a basic economic policy by which courts, executive agencies and Congressional committees would all be guided.

The approach I propose is that, by act of Congress, we make our present limited and essentially negative dogma of competition (such as is embodied in our antitrust laws and their current enforcement) clearly *subordinate* to a broader and more basic proposition. Such a new law should make it explicit that what we want is something positive: productivity for the general welfare and the common defense. The Sherman Act *forbids "restraint* of trade"— a double negative. The new law, by contrast, should expressly *foster* the *"development* of trade"—a double affirmative.

It is my suggestion that we should not attempt a whole array of specific amendments to this and that section of the Sherman Act or the Clayton Act, but rather a broad declaration of public policy that the *prime* concern of Congress is not with competition, per se, nor with competitors, but with productivity and the promotion of an ethical and economic distribution of this productivity. This new statute should then go on to provide expressly that the Sherman and Clayton Acts, and all other existing laws, administrative policies and judicial interpretations of the antitrust laws, as well as consent decrees that are not consistent with or that do not further this Basic Economic Policy, are to that extent modified, set aside or repealed.

The specific terms of such a law would of course have to evolve out of a consideration of the realities about Bigness such as those I have sketched in this writing; it would be necessary in such a law that there be spelled out, in legal terms, well-defined criteria by which to judge whether Bigness furthers or injures the public interest, criteria of the sort I have herein suggested only in laymen's language.

Suppose Congress had passed a Basic Economic Act generally along the lines I have here suggested. Suppose, further, that some large business is thereafter sued by the government, or brought before the Federal Trade Commission. The complaint, let us say, is that as a consequence of its size and its "potential" or actual position in the industry the business is in "restraint of trade," or that it impairs, or potentially impairs, competition, contrary to the antitrust laws. The government seeks to have the defendant enterprise broken into smaller units, or some similar decree entered.

The large company, in presenting its answer, would not, under the new law, be limited to the single issue of the effect on competition either of its size or its practices or business advantages that are a consequence of its size. Nor under such a new law would the legality of Bigness, in the setting of the particular facts, be determined solely by whether, for reasons based upon or growing out of the defendant's size, some competitor (or would-be competitor) has suffered a loss in his business, or fears such a loss.

The issues, while they might include such matters, would be far broader; the facts about the company that would be relevant in its defense would be far more comprehensive.

For under such a proposed Basic Economic Act the legal test Bigness would have to face would thenceforth be whether the particular aspect of size challenged by the government does in fact *further the public interest.* Whether its business acts under question (a merger or acquisition, for example, or its relations with customers or suppliers or licensees under its patents, etc.) do further the public interest would be judged by the court or tribunal by such measuring rods as the criteria suggested throughout this book, and others of that character. Under the proposed new law when Bigness was challenged in the courts or commissions, or by officers of the executive branch, and presumably before Congressional committees as well, it would be permitted to show, if it could, such affirmative contributions as it has made and is making to the health and vitality and prosperity of the country.

But here I must return to the point made at the very outset of this writing: the need for a change in feeling about Big Business. *With* such a change, the broad test of over-all public interest I here suggest, in lieu of the narrow legalistic test of competition, can bring good results for the country. *Without* a real change in feeling and comprehension, such a new law or a new interpretation of the Sherman Act may be ineffective. If we approach the issue of Bigness in an attitude of grudging acceptance of the inevitable, we commit almost as deep an error as if we dismember it with the meat axe of dogmatic trust busting. We need an *attitude of mind* as affirmative and positive as is this great capability for productivity itself.

The whole problem of promoting the public welfare through Bigness will change once we shift from the negative to the positive—from no to yes.

Such a change is a deep and profound thing. It is simple, but it is not easy. It puts a heavy demand upon the imagination and discipline and judgment of individuals and of a people.

The changes from punishment to education, from domination by force to persuasion and co-operation, from totalitarian dictation to democratic self-government are all examples of this course of human evolution.

Now we are ready for this transition from no to yes with respect to Bigness. We are ready for a frame of mind in which *the things that Bigness can do for us* become our *central* concern: protecting ourselves against the abuses of Bigness become subordinate, a matter delegated to the business police. The dominant note should be finding ways and means of encouraging and safeguarding the principle of growth and development and size so that it can contribute best to the well-being of the country in the new era that now opens.

23

Making Bigness Serve Modern Individualism

THE new era for America is built upon Bigness. This surely is clear. But is it a good era; is it a good society? To many thoughtful people it is not good. And since these are, by and large, men and women who deservedly exert very great influence upon public opinion, emotion and standards of values, and therefore upon both public policy and private decisions, their reservations and their convictions call for earnest consideration.

One can sum up their views in this way:

The society of Bigness is *not* good for two principal reasons: First, it is too "materialistic." Second, it is so complex and gigantic that the individual is reduced to nothing.

Those who hold these views about the state of our culture quite naturally live in an atmosphere of gloom and pessimism, a darkly unhappy outlook engendered not so much by the possibility of World War III (which sobers every sensible man) but a feeling of the deterioration of the moral, spiritual and imaginative fiber of their fellow Americans under the impact of the technical society of Bigness.

It is, of course, quite evident that the writer does not join in these views. Nor in any reasonable perspective can I understand how one can share in this dejected appraisal of the moral and spiritual state of our society, or in the low estimate it makes of our capacity to devise correctives for such evils as centralization, without thereby losing the benefits of size.

On the contrary, I see a hopefulness and a sanguine spirit, a people so imaginative that it has conceived and is maturing this genuinely creative achievement of large-scale but decentralized production and distribution; a people endowed with such sensitivity to social adjustment and such faith in the future as is inherent in our concept of modern government. Moreover, I disagree, profoundly, with the view that our talents for productivity have made us excessively "materialistic," or that the iron embrace of giantism must necessarily suffocate individual uniqueness and self-expression.

The thesis of this book is not merely that Big Business is a superior economic tool by which to provide those *things* that constitute the physical basis of living. What I have endeavored to do is to express my conviction—and the reasons for my belief—that in Bigness we have the material foundation of a society which can further the highest values known to men, values we describe as "spiritual."

We Americans exhibit at times a strong impulse to depreciate our material achievements and our capabilities for productivity and mechanization, tend to be defensive about our "bathtub civilization," about our preoccupation with gadgets and the fascination that physically big things have for us.

There are many among us who are willing to concede, even to insist, that we are too "materialistic" and hence lack the qualities of faith; to agree with our critics that we compare unfavorably in this respect with the more "spiritual" people of the Far East; to compare—to our detriment—our own passion for speed, our money-making and our restless energy, with the poor but assumedly happier and "more contented" peoples of the simpler, less gadget-dependent civilizations of India, or of the South Seas, or of our own pioneer days, or of Elizabethan or Victorian times, or of the days of ancient Greece.

This half-apologetic state of mind is supposed to be especially characteristic of our intellectuals and artists, and of people of a liberal bent. But it is by no means so limited. One finds it quite common, as I have had many opportunities to observe at first hand, among some of the very businessmen, engineers and scientists who are largely responsible for Bigness (which I use here as a more or less convertible term for our industrialized and technical civilization).

This feeling that we are losing our spiritual strength is reflected in the recent words of two quite different American leaders. One is a public-spirited man, long a chief adviser to the world of business, Mr. John Foster Dulles, from whose book *War or Peace* (Macmillan, 1950) I quote:

Something has gone wrong with our nation or we should not be in our present plight and mood. . . . What we lack is a righteous and dynamic faith. . . . Our greatest need is to regain confidence in our spiritual heritage. . . . There is no use having more and louder Voices of America unless we have something to say that is more persuasive than anything yet said.

The second is the great theologian and liberal philosopher, Dr. Reinhold Niebuhr, who writes:

American sanity is threatened not only by the combination of power and insecurity which has become our fate. Our culture is also threatened from within by the preoccupation of our nation with technology. . . . The cultural and spiritual crudities of a civilization preoccupied with technics compare with the pastoral and rustic crudities of a frontier civilization as a neon-lighted movie palace compares with a cow-barn . . . it will require ages of the most sophisticated and the most rigorous and vital kind of criticism to save our American culture from destruction by technocratic illusions, even if it should be saved from physical destruction by atomic explosions.*

This downgrading, as "materialism," of our talents for productivity runs deep in the stream of our minds. It accounts in considerable part, I think, for the negative feeling about business as a vocation, ranging from cynicism or boredom to an immature snobbishness; it accounts in part for an undisguised defensiveness about their life's work that one finds not infrequently among even the most constructive and successful of businessmen.

The general defensiveness about "materialism" stems chiefly from a plain and quite human mix-up (planted in our minds I know not how) between *means* and *ends*. The means are our ability to produce and distribute the material basis of our living. The ends are the use and purpose to which we put these material things.

* *Partisan Review*, May-June, 1952, p. 303.

Walt Whitman, the poet of democracy, sings the song of American idealism and individualism. Like many other perceptive people, of his day and our own, he was not himself particularly interested in money-making. But he did see and speak clearly of the basic part it played in the development of democracy and individualism. Nothing shows better how far our pessimists have wandered from first principles than to reread Walt Whitman's words. Writing some eighty years ago he drew his picture of the future in *Democratic Vistas*, an answer to the ferocity of the critics of the "materialism" of American culture of that day. I quote from a salient passage, and in particular a telling and explicit footnote:

The true gravitation-hold of liberalism in the United States will be a more universal ownership of property, general homesteads, general comfort—a vast, intertwining reticulation of wealth . . . democracy looks with suspicious, ill-satisfied eye upon the very poor, the ignorant, and on those out of business. She asks for men and women with occupations, well-off, owners of houses and acres, and with cash in the bank—and with some cravings for literature, too; and must have them, and hastens to make them. Luckily, the seed is already well sown, and has taken ineradicable root.

And then the poet and dreamer follows with this pungent footnote:

For fear of mistake, I may as well distinctly specify, as cheerfully included in the model and standard of these [Democratic] Vistas, a practical, stirring, worldly, money-making, even materialistic character. It is undeniable that our farms, stores, offices, dry goods, coal and groceries, enginery, cash accounts, trades, earnings, markets, etc., should be attended to in earnest, and actively pursued, just as if they had a real and permanent existence. I perceive clearly that the extreme business energy, and this almost maniacal appetite for wealth prevalent in the United States, are parts of amelioration and progress, indispensably needed to prepare the very results I demand. My theory includes riches, and the getting of riches, and the amplest products, power, activity, inventions, movements, etc. Upon them, as upon sub-strata, I raise the edifice designed in these Vistas.*

If we suffer from a false snobbishness and lack of perception about the place of "materialism," we are by no means the only ones. The British, many of them, are bitten with the same bug. Thus, in a recent issue of *The New Statesman and Nation* one reads the most critical comments on the unhealthy state of British coal production, with its grave consequences for the defense of Britain. The editors find it "difficult to deny" that this state of affairs is caused not by lack of funds "but by a lack of men capable of conceiving and carrying out reorganization of pits and coal fields," in other words, competent business executives. Then in an adjoining column of the same issue some dignified fun is made of American preoccupation with business, recalling that a hundred years ago the "urbane Frenchman," Alexis de Tocqueville visiting America said, "I know of no country, indeed, where the love of money has taken stronger hold on the affections of men." The editors agree the analysis still stands: "One hundred-odd years of technological change, war and politics have not rendered obsolete these insights into American civilization."

* *The Portable Walt Whitman,* Viking Press, 1945 (ed. Mark Van Doren), p. 416, 417.

Another British instance. Mr. Herbert Morrison, lately Foreign Secretary, recently criticized a proposal that sponsored television be permitted, as contrasted with the exclusive government-operated radio and television of the B.B.C., on the ground that commercial broadcasting would be "totally against the British temperament, the British way of life, the best or even reasonably good British traditions." Which drew from Mr. George Schwartz the candid and relevant observation that Mr. Morrison's words

will raise a great laugh in the rest of the world which for centuries has seen the British mercantile marine thrust its prow into every corner of the globe. There may be other and sound reasons for objecting to sponsored broadcasting, but it is too late in the day to turn our backs on commercialism. If we had enjoyed a peaceful world since 1913 we might have pretended by now that grandfather had never been in the ironmongery. We might have become a race of gentlemen farmers patronizing the arts and supporting a vast retinue of aesthetes. As it is, we are right back in the ironmongery and haberdashery business and 50,000,000 people have to live by selling the stuff.*

A first cousin of the notion that our technical society is a debased kind of civilization because it is materialistic is the criticism that this society is neither creative nor imaginative. To support this indictment it is said that simpler societies produced great poets, painters, sculptors, musicians, playwrights and actors, whereas our time is lacking in those qualities of towering artistic imagination which are the true and only measure of a civilization.

Admitting that, as we see them today, contemporary

* George Schwartz, in the London *Sunday Times,* quoted by John Crosby, in his column "Radio and Television," New York *Herald Tribune* for July 23, 1952.

artists are not of heroic stature, I wonder if we know just what it is in a society that produces a Shakespeare, a Goethe, a Beethoven, a Praxiteles or a Rembrandt. Do we know enough to agree that there is a close negative correlation between technology and art, or that technology and Bigness cause a blight to fall upon the great artist, when that historically rare genius comes upon the world's stage?

Certainly one must reject both the assumption that the genius of human imagination and spirit is only expressed in the arts, and the notion that whereas the purple sails of the argosies of Tennyson are things of beauty, the silver grace of an airplane in flight is not, because it is "mechanical."

Each epoch of humanity tends to find its own and sometimes quite different ways of expressing what is inspiriting and beautiful. It may be, two hundred years hence, critics of that day will conclude that the imagination of the mid-twentieth century's scientists and engineers and architects was as bold, daring, original and beautiful as we today believe that of the great poets and artists was two hundred years ago. There are many forms of creativeness. In the literary and artistic we are today sadly deficient, if the judgment of today's critics turn out to be right two hundred years hence. But in qualities of scientific and technical originality and fertility, this society of ours cannot be dismissed as other than inspired and imaginative in the highest sense.

One of the major reservations about Bigness, and the society upon which, in a physical sense, it is built, is that it has a blighting effect upon the individual. This objection ranges from the effect of Big Business upon the ability of an individual to begin a business of his own and prosper in it, to the more philosophical but none the less real objection that Bigness tends to destroy the sense of importance, and the freedom to be oneself which are integral to individualism as a tenet of democratic faith.

I recently noted a newspaper advertisement which began:

AN OPEN LETTER

For more than 20 years, it has been my ambition to operate a business of my own, in which I make the decisions, assume all responsibility, and take all the blame.

This announcement of the opening of a new business— in this case a restaurant and cocktail lounge—strikes a very familiar American note and one of central relevance in considering the harmful effects of Bigness upon the individual's independence.

To want to set up in business for himself, to be his "own boss," is as much a part of the American tradition as razzing the umpire, or the Sunday-afternoon nap. The tradition is far from dead: there are over ten million men and women who are their "own bosses," or "active proprietors" in the terminology of the census; these figures do not include farming, which is, of course, the largest independent business group of all.

But there are millions of people who can never expect to set out in business for themselves, or be in a position "to make all the decisions," in the sense of the open letter of the proud new proprietor of Rennie's Old Castle Inn. Bigness is indeed making us more nearly a nation of employees; in some cases several hundred thousand individuals working for the same employer.

As it affects the lives and aspirations of our young men and women particularly* it is undeniable that this represents what a thoughtful friend of mine has described as "a great break with tradition." Upon graduation from a university, in the twenties, he and some of his friends were recruited for employment with one of our largest and best Big Businesses of a generation ago (as it is still today).

We were dismayed [he writes me], at the vista of mediocre aspiration and of compartmentalized lives. The course of a big business career was predictable and foreclosed. It was also, as the personnel department pointed out, secure. The appeal of graduated salary raises and retirement on a pension was held out as the big lure. But in my high school days the appeal had been to ambition, a good deal was said about achievement and independence.

Have we lost something very precious, since for so many millions "working for yourself" is no longer a possible course? I think we have indeed lost something of great value.

How great is this loss? In the first place, to be realistic, one should remember that it is not everyone by any manner of means who really wants "to make the decisions, assume all responsibility, and take all the blame."

Beyond that, we must keep reminding ourselves of how

---

* For an excellent statement on "Is Big Business a Career?" by One Who Thinks Not (anonymous) see *The Literature of Business.* Harper & Brothers, 1928, p. 31.

many small jobs and businesses—of a kind that never existed before the era of Bigness has brought with it. Today the manufacture of automobiles is obviously not a good place for a man to start to be his own boss. But the automobile has certainly spawned tens of thousands of independent or semi-independent one-man businesses; they can be seen along every highway of this highly mobile land—not only filling stations, small repair shops, vegetable stands and the like, but hundreds of one-building factories that manufacture parts and components of the intricate machinery of a motorcar.

But there are far more important considerations even than these. I refer to the great strides being made in big industry, by management and by labor organizations, to enable individual workers to find a new kind of personal and individual satisfaction in their jobs, that replaces and perhaps in some ways sharpens the old-time satisfactions of independence in the days of small self-owned enterprise.

In the past quarter of a century there has probably been more realistic effort in industry devoted to a better understanding of the worker *as an individual*, and his relations to other individuals, than ever before in history.

In point of fact, the individual human being has become the very center of management's and labor's concern in some of our more progressive huge business undertakings. What is it that gives workers their chief satisfaction? What are the chief causes of their dissatisfaction on the job? How can the relations between men, working together, be improved? How can men find in their work and associations in large organizations and with huge machines the quality of satisfaction and joy which craftsmen of old found in theirs? In their creative effort to demonstrate that "the proper study of mankind is man,"* modern management and unions are laying the foundation of a new individualism.

Largely because of the productivity of Bigness most of man's independence need no longer come from his job directly. Now machines and better management together with a new social opinion and the consequences of labor organizations' efforts have provided workers, in Big Business particularly, with a spectacular increase in leisure, and consequently a proportionate increase in independence. The total percentage of a man's week *which is his own* has markedly increased.

When the hours of labor are cut from sixty a week to forty-four—and we can afford this chiefly because of the new productivity of large-scale industry—we have thereby added sixteen hours to each man's independence every week. In those added hours he is his "own boss," not in the sense of the man who owns his own business, but potentially in an even more meaningful sense.

It is plain that larger units of human organization are the order of the future. As I write, the radio announces that three men have crossed and recrossed the Atlantic within the hours of daylight. More significant even than this physical contraction are the tidal currents that move us irresistibly toward closer contact and greater cohesion

* See Stuart Chase: *The Proper Study Of Mankind*. Harper & Brothers, 1948.

among once disparate peoples, and thereby to larger and larger economic and political units of people, in short, toward Bigness.

What then of the individual, in this trend toward Bigness? There is a general assumption that the bigger the organization the smaller the individual, the less freedom to be himself. My own observation casts doubt upon this proposition. My impression is that the large unit *potentially* provides an opportunity for the flourishing of individuality as great, perhaps even greater than the small unit toward which our backward glances are cast with such an undisguised sense of loss.

Dr. Margaret Mead, the noted anthropologist, is one of a handful of scholars who have closely studied small and simple societies at first hand. Her testimony was impressive, therefore, when at a recent International Symposium on Anthropology, the press reported her as saying that " 'oneness' of the world in the future did not mean that individuality would suffer. She said all the evidence showed that large and complex societies gave much more play to the individual than small groups could afford to give."

We are living in a society in which, for the first time in history, almost all its benefits—physical and nonmaterial—are enjoyed not only by a few at the top but by everyone, all up and down the line. As a measure of the increased value attached to the worth of *all* individuals, this is a profound ethical and spiritual advance. Individualism has reached a new high point in this machine civilization of ours.

The ancient world of Greece and Rome created great art and literature; but this was produced for a limited aristocracy and in a society based upon human slavery. The magnificent castles and cathedrals of the Middle Ages came out of a society of half-starved serfs. The Industrial Revolution of the eighteenth century brought to a few great wealth and political power; but the machine was master for most of the population, and they derived from it only an urban life uglier than the pastoral poverty that afflicted the peasants before them.

Today one finds the physical benefits of our society distributed widely, to almost everyone, with scant regard to status, class or origin of the individual. Much the same is true of such benefits as education, police protection, recreation, health measures, etc., and of such precious nonmaterial benefits as the ability (as well as the right) of the individual in this country to move freely from place to place, or from job to job.

In any judgment upon the place of the individual in our new industrial society of Bigness, such factors as these revolutionary advances must be neither overlooked nor obscured.

The effect of Bigness upon the soul, in short whether it makes for better human beings, is of course a most subtle and complex subject. My qualifications to discuss it with authority are negligible, and I shall touch only its outer dimensions here.

There are those who feel that modern science, technology and machines have not made human beings better. They tend to discount the virtues of physical improvement—housing, sanitation, mobility, refrigeration, communication and so on—which technology and machines have brought the individual.

To those who take this general view, machines and Bigness are virtually one and the same evil. Machines mean Bigness, and both are of doubtful value.

, I encountered this emotion in the Tennessee Valley. When electricity was beginning to find its way into farm homes, or even towns where it had never before been known, there were objections that hill farmers' lives would not be helped but harmed by these conveniences. Such views, however, I never heard from the farmers and their wives of that valley. I noticed that the skeptics of machinery lived in towns and cities, where they had themselves long been surrounded by these mechanical aids.

I have visited the hinterlands of Central America, India, Pakistan, Japan, Siam, Egypt. There I saw primitive living, unaffected by modern machinery or technology; this did much to confirm my feeling that machines and their development provide the greatest opportunity in the whole history of mankind to improve the lot of the individual human being.

The continued contraction of the area in which men's backs do the hard, exhausting drudgery of this country is directly related to Bigness. It is size only that can produce the machinery in quantity and at low enough prices to make this epochal transformation a reality in our time. It has taken Bigness to make these things commonplace in millions of homes instead of confining them to the homes of a few people of means.

Wherever human beings live in utter and hopeless

poverty, wherever they must do work that is exhausting and bestial and unfit for human beings (and this is the rule rather than the exception in many parts of the world today), wherever individuals live in abject insecurity and fear of hunger and exposure and disease, the spirit of such individual is degraded, the dignity of man and the integrity of his individuality as a human being is violated. Hence, it seems to me, wherever Bigness and the machine have alleviated or eliminated such degradation of the human spirit, the inner life of man has, to this degree at least, been enriched and nourished.

There was an old dream: the independent man in his own little shop or business. It *was* a good dream.

There is a new dream: a world of great machines, with man in control, devising and making use of these inanimate creatures to build a new kind of independence, a new awareness of beauty, a new spirit of brotherliness.

The brain of man conceived these fabulous machines, and the intellect of man can master them to further the highest purposes of human freedom and culture.

Bigness can become an expression of the heroic size of man himself as he comes to a new-found greatness.

INDEX

acrilan, 62
Adams, Henry, 37 q.*
Adelman, M. A., 140 q.
advertising, 93; effect on innovation, 94
agriculture, 122 ff.
Air Reduction, 79
Aluminum Company of America, 59
American Capitalism, Galbraith, 74 q.
American Cyanamid Co., 125
American Silver Co., 142
American Tel. & Tel. Co., 63, 102, 104
Anaconda Copper Co., 59
A & P, 116, 161
Arvin, Newton, 37 n.
atomic bombs, 100 ff.
Atomic Energy Commission, 42, 72, 100 f., 152, 174
Auto Workers Union, 19

Babcock & Wilcox Co., 160
Bank of America, 120 f.
banking, 16 f.; branch, 120 f.
banking and credit, advantages of bigness in, 119-121; competitive nature of, 16, 17
Bell System, 92, 102 ff., 155
Bergson, Herbert A., 172 q.
Berle, Adolf A., Jr., 23 ff. q., 140 q.
Big, definition of, 35
Big Government, not inevitable, ix

*q.=quoted

Borden's, 79
Brain Trust, 25
Brandeis, Justice Louis D., 41 q., 143 q.
Brookings Institution, 11
bureaucracy in business, 156-163
business, as vocation, 192; creativeness of, 3, 31, 193; distrust of, 4, 97
business machines, electronic, effect on management, 67

Celanese Corporation of America, 74 ff.
centralization, 151-155
Centre Technique des Industries de la Fonderie, 90
chain-store system, 116 ff.
Chase, Stuart, 200 n.
chemical industry, entry of new firms, 75 ff.; potentialities, 8
Clayton Act, 23, 33, 168, 170, 184, 185
coal industry, diversification in, 77; effects of competition from substitutes, 61
Coca-Cola, 89
Collier's Magazine, 72 n.
color television, 162 f.
Columbia Broadcasting Co., 162
Commerce, Department of, 141; Business Advisory Council of the, 11

Commonwealth Edison, 112
competition (*see* New Competition);
    internal, 91 ff.; and research (*see*
    research); term defined, 54
Conant, President James G., 71 q.
Cordiner, Ralph J., 154 f. q.
Corn Products Co., 79
costs, and monopoly, 51; of distribu-
    tion, 117
cotton, 61, 63
countervailing power, 55

dacron, 62
decentralization, governmental, need
    for, 16; in business, methods, 153
    ff.; TVA as demonstration of, x
Democratic Vistas, Whitman, 193
    f. q.
Diamond Match Co., 81 f.
Diesel engine, 69
distilling, 76
distribution of goods and credit,
    114-121
diversification, 73-80
Dobbs hats, 92
Douglas, Mr. Justice, 4 n., 173 q.
Dulles, John Foster, 191 f. q.
Du Pont, 35, 69, 78, 79, 177
Durez Plastics, 84

Eagle Picher, 78
Economic Development, Committee
    for, 11
economic power, 22 ff.; of labor
    unions, 135; of military services,
    134; studies of concentration of,
    23-25
Economic Report, Joint Congres-
    sional Committee on the, 136
economists, criticized, 55 ff.
electrical energy, 110 ff.
employers, power of, 20

farms, 122 f.
Federal Communications Commis-
    sion, 103, 162

Federal Trade Commission, 38 q.,
    41, 49, 139, 169, 170, 184, 186
fertilizers, 124
Food Machinery and Chemical
    Company, 79
Ford, Henry, 53 q.
Ford Foundation, 11
Ford Motor Company, 83 f., 85
Forest Products Research Labora-
    tory, 126
forests, 125 ff.
Fox, John N., 157 q.
Frankfurter, Mr. Justice, 163 q.
free enterprise, and freedom of
    choice, 40, 47; workers committed
    to, 18
"Free the Atom," Lilienthal, 72 n.
freedom of choice, and Bigness, 40

Galbraith, Professor, 74 q.
General Electric, 35, 70, 87, 89, 141,
    154
General Motors, 26, 85, 89, 91, 108 f.
glass, 65
Glidden, 78
government, new role of, 14-17
Great Britain, 115, 120
Great Depression, 26

Hand, Judge Learned, 6, 50 q.
Hanna interests, 77
Harriman, Edward H., 145
Hat Corporation of America, 92
Hickenlooper, Senator, 174
highway system, remaking of, 9
Holman, Eugene, 133 q.
Holmes, Mr. Justice, 168 q.
Hughes, Charles Evans, 41
human relations, concern of big in-
    dustry, 199

Illinois Bell, 92
individualism, modern, 189-204
Industrial Revolution, 202
inefficiency, 156-163
insecticides, 124 f.

insurance companies, financing by, 134
integration, 81-87
Interior, Department of, 130
International Minerals and Chemical Corporation, 129
Interstate Commerce Commission, 64
Interstate Compact Commission, 130
iron & steel industry, changes in, 110
"Is Big Business a Career?," 198 n.

Jones & Laughlin, 85
Justice, Department of, 49, 59; Antitrust Division of the, 103, 169, 170, 172 q., 175, 184

Knox hats, 92
Krilium, 69, 125

labor relations, and large enterprises, 107 ff.
Lewis, John L., 19
liberalism, and change, xi; and wealth, 193; attitude toward "materialism," 191 ff.
Liquid Carbonic, 79
Literature of Business, The, 198 n.
London Economist, 90 q.
London *Sunday Times,* 195 q.

management, and New Competition, 26-31; effect on, of antitrust suits, 5, 104; new kind of executive, 26-28; self-perpetuation, 157
Manhattan District, 72, 101
Material Policy Commission, 126 f. q.
materialism, 192 ff.
Mead, Dr. Margaret, 201 q.
Means, Gardiner C., 23 f. q.
mergers of competitors, 178
Mickey Mouse, 121
mineral resources, 112 f., 129
minerals, basic, 112 f.

Mines, Bureau of, 72
Minute Maid Corporation, 157
Modern Corporation and Private Property, The, Berle, Means, 23 ff. q.
monopoly, by government, 71
Monsanto Chemical Company, 69, 125
Montgomery Ward, 116
Morrison, Herbert, 195 q.
Moses, Robert, 9
Muscle Shoals, 58, 124

National Dairy, 79
National Electric Light Assn., 149
National Lead Co., 78
National Petroleum Council, 130
National Research Council, 174
national security, 98-105; needs, 21 f.
natural resources, conservation of, 122-130
New Competition, 26, 47, 48, 56 ff., 60, 65, 68, 74, 77, 80, 81, 83, 86, 88, 91, 94, 147, 150
New Deal laws, 25
New Statesman and Nation, The, 194 q.
Niebuhr, Dr. Reinhold, 192 q.
Norris, George, 42
Norris Dam, 111
nylon, 62, 69, 79

oil industry, competition with coal, 61; conservation policies, 129; international cartel charges, 130
Oil Trust, 145
Oldsmobile, 91
oligopoly, 54
organized labor, changed role of, 17-20
orlon, 62

Pacific Gas and Electric, 112
paint, 78
Partisan Review, 192 q.
Pecora investigation, 41

penicillin, 76
Penick and Ford, 79
Penney Stores, 116
pension funds, dangers, 135
Pittsburgh Coke and Chemical Co.,
    124
Pittsburgh Consolidated Coal Co.,
    68 f. q., 77
Pittsburgh Plate Glass Co., 78
power, concentration of, 138-150
Pratt & Whitney, 143
Prices, uniformity as evidence of
    monopoly, 50
productivity, and Bigness, 109 ff.
Proper Study of Mankind, The,
    Chase, 200 n.
"Public Responsibilities of Big
    Companies, The," Holman, 133 q.

radio, 63
Radio Corporation of America, 87,
    89, 162 f.
"Radio and Television," Crosby,
    195 q.
railroads, regulation of, 64 f.
Republic Steel Company, 160
research, and agriculture, 123-125;
    and forestry, 125-128; and small
    business, 69-70; by Government,
    quality of, 71; factor in New Com-
    petition, 68; importance of Big-
    ness for, 68-72
Reuther, Walter, 19
R. F. C., 17
Roosevelt, Franklin, 23, 25, 41, 42,
    145 q.
Roosevelt-Hoover contest, 24
Roosevelt, Theodore, 41, 62, 70,
    145 q.

Sarnoff, General David, 63
Schenley Laboratories, Inc., 76
Schuman-Monnet Coal-Steel Plan,
    90
scientific research, *see* research

Sears Roebuck & Company, 26, 116,
    118
security, individual, 105-109
Security and Exchange Commission,
    135
*Selected Letters of Henry Adams,
    The,* 37 q.
Sherman Antitrust Act, 23, 33, 34,
    37, 42, 43, 62, 64, 70, 87, 88, 103,
    145, 168, 170, 172, 173, 176, 177,
    184, 185, 187
Sherwin-Williams, 78
small business; advantages over big,
    141 ff.; and concentration, 36, 140-
    141; and industrial research, 69-70;
    creation of, by Bigness, 36, 118,
    142, 199; credit needs and big
    banking, 119; critical of Bigness,
    136; "curse of smallness," 143 ff.;
    essential nature of, x; govern-
    ment subsidy of, 144-145; im-
    provement of management, 118;
    labor policies of, 144; not the
    norm, 6; numbers of, 140 ff.; ver-
    sus Big, 36
socialism, consequence of Bigness,
    147 ff.
soil conditioners, 125
spiritual values, 39, 190
Staley, A. E., 79
Standard Oil Company (N. J.), 89,
    133, 142
sterility in business, 156-163
Supreme Court, 104, 162, 173 q.
synthetics, 62, 63
Systox, 124

Taft, Senator Robert A., 136 f. q.
television, 66, 70; color, 162 f.
Temporary Economic Committee,
    41
Timberg, Sigmund, 6 q.
titanium, 78
Tocqueville, Alexis de, 194 q.
"Toward the Industrial Atomic
    Future," Lilienthal, 72 n.

transportation, competition of alternatives in, 64 f.
Truman, President, 102, 139 q., 146
trust busting, 167-181
TVA, 42, 58, 72, 100, 111, 112, 124, 152
TVA: Democracy on the March, Lilienthal, 152 q.
Twentieth Century Fund, 11

underdeveloped countries, and products of agricultural research, 125; need for technology in, 203-204; weakness of distribution system in, 114-115
Union Carbide, 35, 79
United Aircraft Corporation, 142 f.
United Auto Workers, 108
United Kingdom, talent for Bigness, 34

U. S. Steel, 35, 106 f., 136

Vanderbilt, Commodore, 145
Veblen, Thorstein, 6

Wall Street, 41
War or Peace, Dulles, 191 f. q.
weed killers, 124
Western Electric, 102 f.
Westinghouse, 87
Weyerhaeuser interests, 126
Whiskey Trust, 145
Whitman, Walt, 40 q., 193 f. q.
Willkie, Wendell, 111 q.
Wilson, Charles, 108, 109 q.
Wilson, Leroy, 102 f.
Wilson, Woodrow, 41
Wisconsin Telephone Co., 92
wood pulp, 82
wool, 61, 63